HOW TO RUN COMMITTEES AND MEETINGS

By the same author

Power and Politics in the School System: A Guidebook
Traditions and Controls in the Making of a Polytechnic:
Your Local Education (*with John Pratt, Ralph Allemano and
Tyrrell Burgess*)
A Guide to Learning after School (*with John Pratt*)

HOW TO RUN COMMITTEES AND MEETINGS

A Guidebook to Practical Politics

Michael Locke

© Michael Locke   1980

First published 1980 by
THE MACMILLAN PRESS LTD
London and Basingstoke
Companies and representatives
throughout the world

Printed in Hong Kong

British Library Cataloguing in Publication Data

Locke, Michael, *b. 1943*
　　How to run committees and meetings
　　1. Meetings
　　2. Parliamentary practice
　　I. Title
　　658.4′56　　　　　　AS6

ISBN 0–333–27053–3
ISBN 0–333–29035–6 Papermac

Contents

Acknowledgements   ix

1. The nature of committees and meetings   1
  1.1   Introduction   1
  1.2   Rules and procedures   6
        Constitutions   6
        Standing orders, rules and conventions 7
        The sources   8
  1.3   Constitutional and collective action 10
        Legitimacy   11
        Collective decisions 13
        Participation and representation 16
        A framework   19
2. Roles and responsibilities   21
  2.1   Committee and officers   21
        Powers and duties 21
        Composition   23
  2.2   Chair   26
        Conduct of meetings 28
        Political leadership 35
        Alternatives   39
  2.3   Secretary   41
        Before the meeting 43
        In the meeting   49
        After the meeting 52
        Wider roles   53
  2.4   Treasurer   55
        In meetings   58
        The organisation   60
  2.5   Other officers   63
        In the meeting   64
        In the work of the association 64

2.6	An ordinary member	65
	For	66
	Against	68
	Out of it	70
3.	Procedure	74
3.1	Principles	74
	The rules	74
	Behaviour	77
	Meetings and committees	81
3.2	Calling a meeting	82
3.3	Agenda	84
3.4	Minutes	91
	Contents	92
	Taking and agreeing minutes	94
	Writing minutes	96
3.5	Quorum	99
3.6	Motions and amendments	100
	Procedure	101
	The basic structure	102
	Is it in order?	106
3.7	Procedural motions	107
	Closure: that the question be put	108
	Next business	109
	Previous question	109
3.8	Voting	110
	Methods	111
	Some complications	114
	The chair's vote	115
3.9	Elections	116
	Nominations	116
	Voting	118
3.10	Subcommittees and reports	120
	Receiving reports	121
	Information and recommendations	124
3.11	Additional controls	126
	Point of order	126
	Point of information	128
	Challenging the chair	129
	Suspending standing orders	130
	Adjourning the meeting	131

	3.12	Disorder	132
		The chair's authority	132
		The rules	134
		Adjourning the meeting	134
		The law	134
		Notes	136
4.	The law and other public controls		138
	4.1	Getting it right	138
		Public watchdogs	144
	4.2	The legal bases of action	145
		Unincorporated associations	146
		Trustees	147
		Charitable status	149
		Ultra vires	151
	4.3	Constraints on meeting, talking and making money	152
		Meetings	153
		Association	154
		Defamation	154
		Fund-raising	156
		Notes	157
5.	Action		159
	5.1	People	159
		Involvement	159
		Tasks and roles	160
		Keeping going	164
	5.2	Decisions	166
		Information and instruction	168
		Levels of decision-making	172
		Kinds of decisions	176
	5.3	Politics	178
		References	182
		Further reading	183
		Glossary and index	185

Acknowledgements

If we have met during these couple of years when I was preparing this book, the chances are that I have picked your brains. The whole idea began in a conversation with a stranger in a railway carriage, and since then all sorts of conversations, idle chats in pubs and parties, have provided ideas and raw material. For the opportunity to talk about the nitty-gritty of politics, the unfamiliar details of procedure, the specialised tactics, pressure groups, unions, local authorities, political bodies of all kinds, the finances of Sikh temples, Swedish styles of management, the Javanese concept of consensus, community politics in North Kensington, I am really grateful. If we have served on a committee together, I am grateful for the opportunity to have learnt from your skills and to have shared enthusiasms, frustrations and even boredom. Most of all, if you have been involved, like me, in the Westway Nursery Association and North Kensington Amenity Trust, I hope you find this book worthy of what we have been through together, the marathon meetings, the triumphs, the struggles that continue – I could not have written this book without you.

I have relied enormously on friends to check points and to read drafts. In particular for their help in the finished product I would like to record my indebtedness to: Mary Locke, who has read and discussed all of several drafts, sustaining the book with criticisms and ideas; Bobby Vincent-Emery; Fred Short; Anil Kumar; Alan Munton (for the literary touch of pointing out *Antony and Cleopatra*); John Winckler at Macmillan (if I still sound like a retired clergyman, it is not his fault); Winifred Carter (for typing and preparing the typescript). None of them, of course, are responsible for what is written.

All these people, and my gratitude to them, are real, but I must make plain that the illustrative examples used in the book (other than the specific legal cases in Chapter 4) do not refer to actual events. Nor do the characters correspond to actual people; I have tried to make this doubly clear by using names which are not those of people with whom I have served on committees, and, though this was not completely possible, in no way do I intend to refer to particular people. The illustrative examples and characters are fictions which I have invented to typify situations. If they sound familiar, it is only because we have been through this agenda so many times before, and no doubt will do so again.

M.L.

1 The nature of committees and meetings

1.1 INTRODUCTION

Many of us could easily spend five evenings a week in committees and meetings – in tenants' associations or local authorities, in action campaigns or professional bodies, in trade unions or school governors, in self-help organisations, political parties or all kinds of pressure groups and voluntary associations. And those who attend as part of their work (or who don't need the money) would not find it difficult to fill up the afternoons and the odd morning as well.

Some people treat these meetings like an amusement arcade of power. But most of us, I suppose, have a serious purpose, whether we achieve it through grinding inch-by-inch advances or have to fight desperate rearguard actions against the disasters of other people's power. Usually, we are concerned at least partly with just keeping going, with maintaining the organisation.

Many more of us are less involved – maybe we have better things to do with our time or maybe nobody will vote us on to a committee. We attend, say, a meeting a month of the committee which runs a housing association or a club. Or we get caught up in a rush of meetings for an instant campaign on, say, the state of the school's lavatories or a plan to build a shopping centre.

We are apologetic about going to committees and meetings. . . . I know it sounds a waste of time but so-and-so expects me to be there. . . . A lot of it will be boring but the plans for relocating the statue of Queen Victoria are coming up for discussion. . . . If we admit that we actually *want* to attend, we are suspected of a ruthless quest for personal power or, worse, do-gooding.

The committees and meetings do not always work well. They waffle; they wrangle for hours and agree nothing; in the confusion

1

they take a ridiculous decision. Everybody has their stories of what went wrong when. . . . ; how, say, Nigel and Reg tore each other's eyes out; how Jo blew it by mentioning the Red Lion meeting; how Gerry won't shut up; how can they be so ignorant, so intransigent, so plain daft. . . .

So we often treat committees and meetings as though they were an aberration from our real, individual lives of work and leisure. But it is such committees and meetings which make possible most of our public life and group or collective activities. They are where the decisions are made to take action, to spend money, to do this rather than that. National and local government is based on people meeting, often in committees. Public bodies, charities and voluntary associations are headed by committees of some kind. Companies are run by boards of directors, which are committees. Trade unions are run through branch meetings, executive committees and general meetings.

Pressure groups are led by committees of enthusiasts — sometimes they aren't much more than a committee. The cricket club, the drinking club, the constituency political party, all have their peculiar versions of committees and meetings. The new opportunities to participate in running our lives — school governing bodies, community health councils and as workers on boards of directors — usually end up as sitting on some kind of committee.

The decision to drive a motorway across our backgarden was taken by a committee, and when we mobilise against it we shall probably form a committee to organise ourselves.

Committees and meetings are simply methods of bringing people (and their different interests) together to consider problems and make decisions. To do this, there is general agreement about the way they should be conducted. Rules have been devised which establish structures and formal procedures. In some organisations these rules are written in constitutions, 'rule-books' or 'standing orders' but many organisations adopt the conventions almost unconsciously.

The rules and conventions can be applied in widely different ways. One meeting may work entirely through formal resolutions, set speeches, written reports and recommendations from committees or subcommittees, with elaborately conducted votes. The person who is chairing the meeting behaves almost like a judge, and everyone speaks with self-conscious formality

Mr Chair, may I support the motion proposed by the delegate. . . .

But another meeting may take a fairly informal approach. The agenda reads, say, 'Report on cooperation with borough council' and the chair starts the item with

Julia, you were asked to nobble your tame councillor.

From this an orderly conversation leads to a consensus about what to do next. Perhaps only if there was a sharp disagreement would that meeting adopt a more formal style and take a vote on a motion. Nonetheless, it has an underlying structure and code of behaviour which are based on the general conventions about the conduct of meetings and committees.

The procedure can sound pompous and unnecessary. But at minimum it is a structure to fall back on when ordinary conversation and rational argument have worn out. A casual meeting can get stuck in the rut of an argument or get nowhere because each faction blocks everyone else's ideas, and then it can be helpful for the chair to ask for a formal motion to be proposed, to conduct an organised debate and take a vote (see 3.6). Sheer weight of numbers or strength of personalities can overwhelm an opposing view until a clear procedure is adopted. A friendly committee can disintegrate into a shambles of separate conversations until the chair says 'I am in the chair and I am going to conduct this meeting according to the rules'.

A larger, public meeting may have no real alternative to formal procedure – other than chaos. It needs the chair to have visible authority; it needs a clear order of business; it needs the business divided up. If we are just presented with the question

What shall we do about the camels?

people get all sorts of ideas, and the discussion wanders all over the place. Whereas when there is a motion that

The camels be bartered for a new treasurer

we have a tangible proposal to deal with.

I am not claiming that all meetings have – or need – such

structure. Brain-storming sessions, therapy groups, conscious-ness-raising groups, sales conferences, etc all use different kinds of conventions – just try raising a 'point of order' in a T-group. And there are different forms of collective decision-making, including management teams, revolutionary cells, spontaneous working groups. This book is not about these kinds of meetings.

This book
This book is about committees and about meetings which are based on formal procedure, its rules and its conventions – albeit, that in many organisations they are used almost unconsciously. In the rest of this chapter I shall stake out the principles of this formal procedure, the rules and conventions: what do they consist of?; what is their rationale?; in other words why have committees?

Chapter 2 considers the roles and responsibilities of officers – chair, secretary and so on – and the ordinary members. In doing so, it goes beyond actual formal procedure and draws on what are, I think, widespread agreements about the way the jobs are effectively performed. Chapter 3 is about the procedure itself, from the principles which underlie the whole through to the detailed points. Chapter 4 sets out how meetings and committees have to work within the law and within other public controls. Chapter 5 suggests how committees and meetings can be encouraged to work effectively.

The book is written so that it can be dipped into for specific points or can be read as a continuous narrative. Thus, readers in a hurry for the practical meat might skip the rest of this chapter, returning later to fill in the foundations.

This book is pitched at the person who is not a constitutional wizard. I have most in mind those people involved in pressure groups, community associations, school governors, local trade union branches and political parties, and other voluntary associations. The descriptions of conduct and procedure for meetings and committees apply generally, however, to all sorts of bodies, though they may have more specialist functions and more expert members. My focus – and motivation – is the ordinary decision-making meeting or committee which affects our work, leisure and place in society.

Meetings or committees

Before I proceed, however, I have to clear up an issue which will seem pedantic: a technical distinction between a *meeting* and a *committee*.

Basically, a *committee* has a limited membership which has been elected or appointed to perform specified functions. A *meeting* consists potentially of all members of an association or of their representatives. Generally speaking, a meeting is the top body which delegates some of its functions to committees. Committees may be 'standing committees' which are established for long-term and regular tasks with delegated powers to act or advisory functions; they may be 'special committees' set up to do a job and then dissolved. Subcommittees are a lower rank of committees to which committees in turn pass down some of their functions.

The procedure at meetings and committees may be different, as I discuss in Chapter 3.1. Meetings are likely to be conducted more formally than committees. In a meeting, for example, you may be required to stand up if you speak and may only be permitted to speak once to each – formally proposed – motion, whereas a committee of the same association may be more relaxed. One model is the House of Commons where its meetings adopt a formal procedure for their debates (set speeches, 'Mr Speaker', 'Honourable Member' etc) but its 'select committees' consist of MPs sitting round tables talking more-or-less normally and the 'committee stages' of bills consist of detailed, to-and-fro discussions.

Trade unions also distinguish between meetings (annual, delegate and branch) and committees. The branch meeting may take place once a month, but the executive committee may meet once a week. In many voluntary associations, pressure groups and community associations the distinction appears rather different. The only meetings are the annual general meeting and special general meetings, whereas what people call 'monthly meetings' may be strictly speaking its committee, and more frequent meetings may be subcommittees of this committee.

Thus, the ordinary citizen might go to a monthly *meeting* of a trade union, a monthly meeting of a tenants' association which is its executive *committee* and a meeting called by a pressure group which is, say, a special general *meeting*. If they were all strictly conducted, the procedures would be different in the *meetings* and the *committees*.

Although constitutional wizards could get worked up about this distinction, I think for most practical purposes it is not noticeable. We deal with a continuum from some meetings which are conducted most formally through to others which are very relaxed – and the difference shows up as much in the styles of different associations as in the technical distinction between meetings and committees. The regular meetings in which we are involved in decision-making might technically be either meetings or committees.

I shall not therefore make the distinction between meetings and committees except where necessary and obvious. In places I do set the formal version in terms of *meetings* and then indicate that it is relaxed for *committees*, but otherwise I use the words inter-changeably, as most people do.

Just for the record: under an erudite point of company law a meeting can very occasionally consist of one person.

1.2 RULES AND PROCEDURES

The ways in which committees and meetings are conducted are based both on written rules and on generally accepted conventions. This section discusses their bases and origins.

CONSTITUTIONS

An association or organisation requires a statement of its existence and its purpose. (This may sound like the beginning of a deep theological or metaphysical dispute but it is a simple constitutional point.) The statement can take many different forms. A limited company, for example, has a memorandum of association which states its name, its objects and its nature (in terms of liabilities and share capital), and this provides the legal basis of its operation and the information for people who might subscribe to it or trade with it. A school governing body has an instrument of government, which states its composition, and articles of government, which state its functions. A local authority committee has a statement of the powers delegated to it by the local council.

Likewise, voluntary associations and political parties have a 'constitution' which begins with a statement of its name and its objects. As with a limited company, the objects clause gives it the power to act in pursuance of those objects – and limits its actions to those objects. A constitution usually includes these main points: name; objects; functions of officers and committees; arrangements for appointing or electing them; provision for membership (and expulsion); arrangements for general meetings; how the constitution can be amended; how the association can be dissolved; and other major rules for the conduct of the association and its meetings.

I discuss how the constitution underlies the procedure of a meeting in Chapter 3.1 and the legal issues in Chapter 4.

Some associations have rule-books which include the broad constitutional statements and the detailed rules, but often associations separate the constitution from the standing orders.

STANDING ORDERS, RULES AND CONVENTIONS

Bodies such as trade unions, local authorities, political parties and some long-established voluntary associations have detailed rules or standing orders. These standing orders may be very intricate; a knowledge of their ins-and-outs can be a tactical weapon in debates. The ability to trip the chair over a point of procedure, to manoeuvre amendments on a motion or to stage-manage the order of speakers can be crucial.

It can get obsessional. Some meetings are beyond comprehension unless you know the rules off-by-heart. They twirl through motions and amendments like a much-rehearsed quickstep without pausing for explanations. Members sweat and sulk about a 'reference back' or 'next business'. You ask 'I'm sorry – can you tell me what's happening', and a wise guy mutters to his mates 'Is that a point of information?' and they guffaw among themselves. You try to speak, and the chair says 'That's out of order' or 'We've completed that item' and shuts you up. Like playing chess without you knowing the rules.

Other bodies, like pressure groups, sports clubs and community associations, do not usually have such detailed rules. They have a few basic standing orders, include the main points in the constitution or rely on the unwritten conventions. They accept the authority of the chair to run the meeting and have evolved the way in which they usually do things. They very seldom refer specifically to rules about the conduct of meetings. To listen to the meeting is like listening to an orderly conversation. Occasionally a problem crops up. Somebody objects to what the chair has done; what can he do about it? The vote is equal for both sides; can the chair vote? A controversial topic is raised without being on the agenda and some members think that it is an attempt to steamroller them; do they just get flattened? The speaker is telling lies; can I interrupt? Then, if there are rules or standing orders, you refer to them. If not, then in most cases you can draw on well-accepted, much-used conventions about debating practice and the procedure of meetings.

THE SOURCES

Although there are differences of style and detail about procedure, the principles are widely recognised. Where do these conventions come from?

The House of Commons practice
The principal source is the procedure of the House of Commons as it has been evolved over the last 500 years. This is the basic outline of the procedure for debating motions and amendments and of most conventions. For parliamentary purposes it is codified in Erskine May (Lidderdale 1976). The basic, nineteenth century textbook, which has been revised frequently since, *The chairman's handbook* by Sir Reginald Palgrave (Palgrave 1964), draws heavily on parliamentary procedure.

Closest to the House of Commons is the school or college debating society (the Oxford and Cambridge University 'Unions', for example) which puts its mind to motions such as

This house believes that a policeman's lot is not a happy one.

This has been turned to more practical purposes as I shall describe in Chapter 3. Likewise, the House of Commons' practice on speaking through Mr Speaker (the chair) rather than person-to-person is generally adopted. So too is the expectation of 'parliamentary language' (see 3.1). Even the fun of calling each other 'the Honourable Member' is copied in references such as 'Our Comrade' and 'The Sister'; often one says 'the previous speaker' rather than naming the person (and not simply because you have forgotten their name).

Trade union rules

Trade unions and labour movements have developed from parliamentary practice their own, now parallel conventions. They have codified procedure into what are often very detailed rulebooks attempting to foresee all manner of circumstances in which different points of view would need to be democratically discussed. The masterwork, *ABC of chairmanship* by Lord Citrine (Citrine 1952), provides an authoritative textbook for such bodies.

Local government law

Another important source for general conventions is the law on local government. Unlike the two previous sources, this has the power of law – on local authorities – and includes detailed provisions on, for example, chairmanship, quorums.

Company law

Likewise, company law, enshrined in the Companies Acts, lays detailed requirements on many aspects of the conduct and procedure of meetings of companies: notice of meetings; conditions under which motions can be put; quorums; reporting by directors; responsibilities of directors and secretaries. And, like the law on local government, it provides an example which other bodies tend to copy.

Public bodies and watchdogs

Requirements are imposed on associations which are under the aegis of public watchdogs such as the Charity Commissioners and the Housing Corporation. These do not have the force of law – though when dealing with the Charity Commissioners it is hard to tell where the law ends and their view of civilisation takes over – and are less detailed but include expectations that meetings will be conducted fairly according to normal conventions. Some agencies do have specific requirements on procedure for meetings and constitutional business.

The law

Permeating everything else is 'The Law' itself. There is no specific legislation about the conduct and procedure of meetings (other than the local government and companies acts. mentioned above), but the courts have ruled on matters which affect the conduct of meetings. Their tendency is to uphold the decisions of properly constituted meetings though they may place 'natural justice' or the judges' ideas above the actual wording of a constitution. I discuss 'The Law' in Chapter 4.

From these traditions, pieces of law and administrative requirements a body of conventions has been built up over the years. These are not rigid or entirely consistent. There are variations – you cannot perform exactly the same in the Oxford Union as in a trade union branch meeting, or in local council meeting as in a community group committee. But the principles and main points are – tacitly – agreed, and associations act according to them (There is nothing mystical about this: all manner of social behaviour and institutional action, including the law itself, is an aggregate of written rules, of precedents, of the ways people have done things in the past alongside conscious decisions to propose certain actions.)

1.3 CONSTITUTIONAL AND COLLECTIVE ACTION

Why does it mean ordinary people sitting around like stuffed shirts spluttering 'If I may, Mr Chair . . . .' or bouncing to their feet to shout 'Point of order' or wading through piles of paper? Why is Mike in the chair acting like god when he's only there because nobody else would do the job?

There are several theoretical reasons, the practical problems of which I shall discuss in the rest of this chapter. The main argument is:

1.   The rules (or conventions) about committees and meetings provide a structure to enable a fair discussion to take place. The structure allows different interests to be represented and different points of view to be put. It provides a neutral framework which allows minorities to be heard. The decisions which they reach are then accepted as legitimate.

Alongside this are two important concepts:

2.   The formal procedure is a way of cutting up business into manageable pieces so that decisions are made item by item, point by point, in logical order, rather than by trying to tackle a great soup of topics all at once.

3.   People in committees and meetings are not just acting as themselves or in their personal interest. They are there in the 'public interest', in the interest of the association or as representatives or delegates of an organisation or constituency. Their responsibility is to the association and its objects rather than to their personal interest.

Another basic concept, which develops from 3., is more contentious:

4.   People are committed to the decisions which they took jointly, and in dealing with other bodies they gain strength from this. The application of this concept ranges from the excuse 'It's not my fault – it was the executive which decided it' through many political shades to a commitment to maintain solidarity on a democratically agreed decision. The application of this varies according to organisations and individual consciences but a basic recognition that the individuals are to some extent committed to collective decisions is crucial.

A further point illuminates some oddities of behaviour in committees and meetings:

5.   The formal procedure depersonalises the discussion. The meeting is controlled by the chair, according to rules or conventions. All statements are directed at the chair, that is, to the meeting as a whole, rather than to individuals as in private conversation. This both removes some of the emotional pressure from discussions and concentrates on issues rather than personalities. (I *am* talking about the theory.)

These concepts are not written down in constitutions, but we should think about them. We are more effective if we appreciate what we are involved in – being on a committee isn't the same as chatting in the front room.

LEGITIMACY

A basic problem of political philosophy is how it is that some people – a few – make decisions on which other people – a large number – act. One answer is that the large number of people are terrified of being shot, hung or imprisoned, and some aspects of some societies operate on this basis. But we need to look further for why people abide by, say, committee decisions in community associations.

The most useful explanations are to do with the concept of

'legitimacy'. People consent to or act in accordance with decisions because they accept that the body had a right to make the decisions. There are different explanations of why:

- we have shared in making the decision;
- we have been represented in making it;
- we acknowledge the power structure of which this body is part.

The effects could be different:

- we obey, if only because we are not prepared for the upheaval of challenging the decision;
- we obey, if only because otherwise we would be punished in a way that the rest of our society or association would accept was legitimate;
- we implement the decision more effectively because we have shared in it or consent to it.

For example, we accept the law of the country partly because we think that parliament has a right to make it and the courts a right to enforce it, partly because we do not wish to be punished and partly because even though we disagree with some part it is not worth a revolution. Moreover, in most of our associations we are not in fear of punishment but willingly recognise the legitimacy of decisions. Perhaps we merely think 'Oh well, we've joined the Corn Dolly Cooperative Society, and that's the way they do things here'.

The concept of legitimacy is interwoven with the issues of the structure of associations, committees and officers. This structure is set out in the association's constitution (or rule-book) with its statement of the powers and duties of meetings, committees and officers. The constitution has been agreed by the members either actively by helping write and amend it or passively by joining and thereby automatically accepting its constitution as it exists. Thus, the legitimacy of a decision often rests on the question: was that meeting/committee/officer acting according to the constitution and rules to which we have agreed?

When the chair of a meeting tells me to shut up or the captain says to field at silly point, I do so not because I am afraid he will thump me but because I accept he has a right to make the decision. I accept his position because I voted in the election, approve of the selection committee, or am simply prepared to accept the way things are. The sanction that he might suspend me from membership is as distant as my alternative of joining another club. The operative force is consent rather than fire-power.

Likewise, once a decision has been made, say, to set up a subcommittee to vet applications for membership, we abide by it even though we do not agree with it. We accept the legitimacy of the management committee which made the decision. We do not try to undermine the decision. Repeat after me: 'We do not try to sabotage the decision.' And if we do undermine the decision we are not so dumb that we do not recognise that we are thereby undermining the management committee and the association which it runs – though in some circumstances this may be appropriate.

This principle is only a starting point. If it is to be effective operationally, other principles are involved.

COLLECTIVE DECISIONS

If a decision is only the combined selfishness of those people who have acquired power, we may not accept its legitimacy even though we accept the constitution and structure. We require that the decision has been made in the collective, group or public interest.

People are not just at committees to act as individuals. We are at the meeting in the interests of the association as a whole or of the people who have sent us. There are two sides to this:

– in coming to a decision we do not just think of ourselves;
– in acting on the decision we stand shoulder-to shoulder with everyone else despite our personal interests and intellectual objections.

Not just individuals
It can be obvious we are not just there for ourselves, for example:

– we have been chosen as a delegate of a branch to put its view to a general meeting;
– we have been elected by an association's general meeting to a committee to run a club;

– we have been appointed to a subcommittee to select staff on behalf of the executive committee.

Who would imagine he was just there to make sure his lover got the job or his favourite tipple would flow like water? How can a delegate who has been mandated to vote for a motion at a conference expect to save her political skin if she betrays that trust?

The member of a committee which runs an association has to act in the interests of the association. His selfish interest is not served by the proposal for a disco, but he agrees to it because it fits the policy of the club and its economics. Or fits the interests of the people who sent him or elected him.

How we should act is less clear when we are appointed in the 'public interest' or as, say, staff representative. The concept of the 'public interest' seems to imply that we should be spokesperson for society as a whole, which sounds impossible. I think it means we are expected to speak and vote

– not for our selfish interest (as above),
– not for a totally partisan case, but
– for an objective or elevated view which still may be founded in our group interest.

So, a staff representative speaks on a management committee not just to get promotion for himself and not for staff interests exclusively. He speaks from a staff point of view and puts the staff's side but is prepared to take a more dissociated or rational view. He may agree in the interests of the institution or the public interest in cutting expenditure that staff should be made redundant.

It is a delicate position. He could decide that, now he is one of the people made redundant, his own position is symptomatic of the staff's case, of the misdirection of the whole institution or of the local authority's failure to serve the public interest. Or that any redundancies require his total opposition not at all in his own cause but because of their extreme importance to his constituency. .

The representative of the chamber of commerce on that same management committee does not face these issues personally and starkly. He nonetheless faces the problem of finding the balance of his position. He doesn't stay quiet simply because no commercial interests are involved. He weighs up the interest of his members generally in public expenditure against judgments about the interest of the institution and the rationality of the proposal.

Solidarity
– also known, depending on your politics, as 'collective responsibility', 'corporate responsibility' and 'loyalty'.

Given that the body has reached a decision properly, the members who shared in making it stick by it. Two sets of reasons for this:

– basic decency, being trusted the next time, surviving;
– gaining strength of numbers and unity.

Examples:

– 'collective responsibility' of the Cabinet in this country, the Minister of Energy, say, is expected to represent in public the views agreed by the whole Cabinet;
– directors of a company do not 'rock the boat';
– members of a trade union maintain 'solidarity' so that bosses are faced with a united front and cannot win over a few workers at a time until the action collapses;
– school governors, according to the Auld Report on the William Tyndale schools,
    . . . should act corporately . . . . Whatever the (governors) decide to do, they should decide together, and by vote if necessary, at a properly constituted (governors') meeting. There should be no decision taken by factions of the (governing) body (Auld 1976, p. 272).

The solidarity may be enforced through tribal loyalty, a Stalinist upper-hand or political wisdom.

Questions and doubts
When we enter a committee do we somehow dump our personal convictions and conscience in the cloakroom? And leave the meeting the robot of the collective machine? No, but we should reckon with the conflict between ourselves as individuals and the collective or public interest.

One area of doubt is between our conscience or moral judgment and the collective interest. Even the most determined collectivist at some point may switch to individual conscience and break ranks – when the tanks roll in or the corruption is undeniable. Even the agonising liberals occasionally duck their heads into group decisions. The dominant wisdom in this country emphasises the individual conscience, unless the conscience belongs to a left-winger or the collective responsibility can be described as 'obedience to your betters' or 'team spirit'.

Another area of doubt is in representing an interest. A mandated *delegate* has little choice: either follow instructions or resign. But *representatives* are often less clear about what serves the interests or groups which they represent. How, for instance, does a parent representative on a school governing body represent the views of parents? How do MPs represent their constituents? They are conventionally expected to follow their conscience (which luckily tends to coincide with the views of the party whips) rather than take instructions from the constituency, but they justify the freedom on the grounds that thereby they best serve the interests of the whole constituency. Such freedom and confidence is not given to elected representatives in associations with tougher structures of responsibility.

There are doubts, too, about to whom the representative should be loyal. Although people are put on committees as representatives or nominees of different interests, their legal responsibility may be to the committee rather than their constituency. For example, you could be put on a charity's executive by a community group and find that legally your responsibility is to act as a trustee in the interests of the charity rather than the community group. Or, you could be nominated to a committee by a trade union but be expected to contribute your knowledge and experience to any discussions, not just to chip in when members' interests are threatened.

PARTICIPATION AND REPRESENTATION

In the discussion so far ideas about participation and representation have been never far from the surface. We look to see not only that the body has the right to make the decision and that the decision was made in the public or collective interest, but that we have shared or been represented in making that decision. Or at least, had the opportunity to do so.

Representation and participation are not the same thing. Voting for a representative who then goes off and does what she thinks would be best for you is different from being in there yourself to make your own alliances and say your piece. Sending a delegate instructed to vote in a specific way is different again. Even the concept of representation covers a lot of variety:

- being an MP, a parent representative on a school governing body, the representative of the community on a local association, the nominee of the chamber of commerce on a flag-day committee;
- membership of a decision-making or advisory or consultative body;
- a representative with the full confidence of the people who sent her, a representative who isn't trusted to choose her own sugar-lumps.

Right
It is partly an issue of right, a matter of political philosophy. We have the right to be represented in our national government, a right to be consulted in this decision, a right to share in that, the grassroots have a right to . . . . These are rights which people have argued and fought for, which we continue to assert, which are accepted by our society and which are continually subject to re-adjustment as our society changes. Now we can say we have the right to participate in decisions which at other times of history would have been the right of the sovereign or of our masters to make. We may lose rights which have been accepted only a few years ago. Philosophers may assert that a right follows from the nature of man and society but it is really, I think, the notch that we and our ancestors have hauled ourselves up to.

Openness
It is partly an issue of the quality and effectiveness of decisions. A number of people can contribute more ideas, skills, knowledge and experience than one person. This argument runs counter to much of the dominant wisdom of our society which holds individual vision and executive action to be essential to truth, justice and the British way. Edmund Burke acknowledged the

argument as well as any founding father of the Conservative Party:

> In my course I have known and, according to my measure, have cooperated with great men; and I have never yet seen any plan which has not been mended by the observations of those who were much inferior in understanding to the person who took the lead in the business.

It can be the wide-ranging view of asking people's opinions stated by Burke or a deliberate choice of people with expertise to join in a decision – the representative of a trade union or a professional association. In a meeting or committee we can subject proposals to debate and criticism, thereby testing and improving them. This does not overlook the fact that ideas have been put up by individuals, but there is no better way of improving proposals than having to justify them to others. Research into group action has shown more effective decisions with less error have been made by groups than by the average individual judgments (Strauss and Strauss 1966).

Communication and consultation

Representation or participation is seen as a means of finding out what people want and of communicating information and decisions to them. This aids understanding, freeing processes of decision-making and action. It may be a matter of persuasion as much as sharing in making decisions.

Efficacy

People are more likely to effectively implement a decision if they have shared in making it, possibly because: we recognise it is a better decision for the collective effort; we feel responsible for it; we trust it; we understand it. Systems of participation, far from reducing efficiency, can actually improve it (Pateman 1970).

Education

Enabling people to share in making decisions which affect their lives has – it can be argued – an educational effect, improving them as citizens – and improving their ability to join in other decisions in future.

Accountability
The other side of the coin of representation is that the representatives are accountable to the people who sent them. Successful accountability is the source of the continuing power of representatives (see 5.3).

A FRAMEWORK

The procedure of meetings and committees:

– organises the discussion into a manageable format;
– provides a structure in which the unpowerful are protected and given the opportunity to contribute;
– depersonalises discussion and concentrates attention on issues.

Organisation
First, the business is sorted out into an agenda (see 3.3), which takes item by item in an orderly sequence. Secondly, within an item there are recognised processes for taking motions and amendments (see 3.6) which transforms the mush of people's thoughts and wishes into explicit statements of intention. Add to this the recognised processes for sorting out which body does what, for reporting and for voting. Through all this, the chair has authority, subject to the meeting, to control and help structure the business.

Structure
The principles are:

– all that it requires to put an opinion is to indicate you want to speak, to be called to speak by the chair and the floor is yours;
– anyone can express their views into a motion and submit it for debate;
– anyone can stand for election to an office or a committee;
– the orderly nature of the meeting and the control of the chair make it easier for someone without a big voice or strength of allies to speak up.

By contrast, consider a meeting without formal procedure (and it has advantages – see 5.3), perhaps set up in order to avoid the established power or limitations of a rigid structure. Anyone can speak – but only those who can speak louder than others. Everyone can be subjected to long monologues, whether or not on the subject, unless the others shout louder or sit on them. Informal cliques develop, taking effective power; meetings go the way they pull them; power is only restrained by the consciences of those who have acquired it or the violence of those who have not.

Depersonalising
Everyday argument goes something like

> The trouble with you, Jo, is that all you care about is your bloody kids/greyhounds/rose-bushes/pension fund . . . .

In a committee or meeting it is likely to go

> I fear, Comrade Chair, that our sister's perspective is dominated by . . . .
> Mr. Chairman could I pick up the issues . . . .
> What Jo has said is obviously important to her but I think as a committee we should . . . .

– arguably silly or constructive, devious or straight; on the whole I think it helps.

> Madam Chairman, these are invaluable points that the previous speaker has raised. Clearly, we must not lose sight of such very particular and personal questions and, if I may say so, Madam Chairman, we are all indebted to the young lady for making the case so vividly and, may I say, persuasively. However, I wonder if I may, through you, Madam Chairman, turn the attention of the meeting to the major questions before us . . . .

– but not necessarily.

2 Roles and responsibilities

2.1 COMMITTEE AND OFFICERS

Some people – a dozen, two dozen, maybe more or fewer – are elected or appointed to form a committee. A committee includes a chair and various other officers, such as a secretary, treasurer, deputy chair, membership secretary, publicity officer, political education officer, entertainments secretary, whatever suits the organisation.

POWERS AND DUTIES

The functions of a committee are set out either in a constitution or in a resolution passed by a meeting or a higher level committee. (They are sometimes called 'functions', 'powers and duties' or 'terms of reference'.) Take the – fictional – example of the Fulham Association of Soup for Aristocrats. Its constitution gives the composition and functions of its executive committee:

> The annual general meeting shall elect ten members to an executive committee.
> The executive committee shall direct the policy and management of the association, subject to provisions of this constitution and any resolutions of a general meeting of the association.
> The executive committee shall appoint from among its members a chair and such other officers as it shall from time to time decide.

On the basis of this statement the executive of the FASA runs all the affairs of the association, deciding how soup should be distributed to the distressed aristocrats of Fulham, managing a 'charity shop' to raise funds, controlling finances, and then reports back to the AGM.

At one of its committee meetings it decides it needs more advice about the content of its soup and passes a resolution:

> The executive committee resolves to appoint a subcommittee to study and make recommendations upon the nutritional properties of various recipes for soup. This subcommittee shall be chaired by the deputy chair of the executive committee and consist of three other members. It shall report to the October meeting of the executive committee.

This statement gives the power and duty to the subcommittee to investigate lots of soups and to report back with recommendations upon which the executive committee will come to a decision about the soups it will provide during next winter.

Other associations and organisations see their structure of committees differently. The executive might not be given such wide powers, describing them more specifically as

> to implement the policies agreed at general meetings

and more narrowly as, among other functions,

> to submit estimates of expenditure to the AGM
> to authorise expenditure within the agreed estimates and within a limit of £1,000.

An executive or management committee might be a smaller group which keeps the association running between more regular meetings, as in the case of a trade union branch or a pressure group where meetings of the whole membership were held, say, monthly.

Some organisations have elaborate structures of committees and, below them, subcommittees. Beneath, say, a council of management is a tier of finance and general purposes committee, environment committee and entertainments committee. Beneath, say, entertainments committee is a music subcommittee, a pinball subcommittee and a special subcommittee on buying a donkey. Each committee or subcommittee is given its functions and instructions by the one above and reports back to it (see 3.10).

The constitution or resolution may say how often a committee or meeting must take place – once in each year, at least quarterly, ten times a year, etc.

Decision-making or advisory
Committees are sometimes given powers to make decisions and act on behalf of the association or main body; these are usually referred to as 'delegated' powers. This power may be limited: 'up to £ . . .' or 'within the range of activities agreed by . . .'. Or the committee may be enabled only to advise or make recommendations (see 5.2).

Standing or special
Committees are set up for a specific short-term function; referred to as a 'special committee' or 'ad hoc' committee. It may advise on a soup recipes or inquire into staff management and prepare a report with recommendations. Committees are also set up for regular and continuing functions; referred to often as a 'standing committee'. It may be an executive committee, a staffing subcommittee, a finance committee, entertainments committee etc.

COMPOSITION

The members of a commitee can be:

- elected by a general meeting, ballot of membership, public meeting or higher level committee in the same organisation;
- appointed by another body as its representative or nominee;
- ex officio, that is automatically on the committee because of the post they hold;
- coopted, that is added to the main membership of the committee, commonly by the vote of the committee itself, as a way of drawing in people who would be useful but do not get elected or appointed through the other routes, a way of keeping some flexibility in the membership.

The composition and method of election (see 3.9) are specified in the constitution or rules.

The committee might be in office for a year from AGM to AGM, for a fixed term of years or months or for the period until its specified functions are completed.

The members might come from all these routes. A school governing body usually includes elected representatives of staff and parents, nominees of the education committee, the head-teacher ex officio and perhaps a couple of coopted members.

Some 'committees' are nothing like this. A few people get together for a campaign and appoint themselves into a 'committee'. No wider membership; no general meetings. It is a way of getting off the ground, but you don't represent anyone but yourselves.

Electing officers
The officers may be elected or appointed directly to their posts. The AGM might elect six or seven, 27 or 28, whatever, people to offices. But under some constitutions the committee members are elected or appointed as a group and then sort out among themselves who should hold which office.

The main officers may be elected or appointed separately even if the others are not. The chair may be elected at an AGM if he is seen as the leader of the whole association more than the controller of the committee. The issue raises thorny problems of political theory (populism versus democratic centralism) and poses the question: to whom is the chair accountable, the general meeting or the committee? As well as the practical politics: what happens if the general meeting elects a chair out of sympathy with the committee?; or if the committee elects as chair a great committee-person of whom the membership have never heard? On similar grounds you may elect the secretary (or treasurer) at the AGM or from among the committee, but you may not face such imponderable questions: in some kinds of organisations the secretary (more than the chair) personally carries statutory responsibilities and must be elected by the AGM (see 2.3).

Some committees have their chair or secretary imposed by a superior, or stronger, body. Some on a wobbly political perch, like a joint committee, have the chair selected by a separate process of negotiation.

Committees may consist entirely of the office-holders or comprise a few officers and several ordinary members of committee. Ordinary members may share out the jobs or just sit there, sourly or smugly, while the officers do the work.

Constitutions sometimes have a clause that members who miss, say, four meetings in a row are removed from the committee.

Officers' functions
The constitution may specify the functions of officers:

> The secretary shall attend all meetings of the general meeting and executive committee and shall be responsible for all minutes, agendas and the recording of business at these meetings. He will be responsible for conducting the affairs of the party in accordance with the decisions arrived at from time to time He will also have overall responsibility for matters concerning membership and liaison with branches.

Law relating to companies and local authorities and some similar regulations place legal responsibilities upon some officers, particularly chair and secretary (see 2.3).

Most definitions or expectations of officers' functions are based upon convention and tradition, as I set out in this chapter. But nobody can predict how they will turn out in a particular association: consider the personal strengths and weaknesses of the people, their relationships, the dynamics of the group, the purpose and work of the organisation (see 5.1).

The selection of posts depends on the kind of association (see 2.5). In a local political party membership secretary may be a big job, but in a pressure group non-existent. A cricket club needs a fixtures secretary but not – usually – a political education officer. Under some rules the secretary has legal responsibilities for the financial side, thus cancelling out a treasurer. The selection of posts can be based on the people available. One year the secretary may take minutes, but another year the secretary may be busy and somebody else prepared to volunteer as minutes secretary.

Nor do the officers necessarily behave as I say they should. I have written about the secretary in terms of efficient, machine-like qualities, but you could thrive with a wild dreamer as secretary, forever pursuing exotic projects and pretty sex-objects, so long as a mug took on the secretarial functions. A chair can be effective because she is a good group leader even though hopeless in public, or vice versa, so long as the group is flexible enough to fill in the gaps. The publicity officer, the membership secretary, the entertainments secretary and the newsletter editor may all fail to do their jobs, so long as the chair and secretary pick up the pieces.

In this chapter I take the main officers section-by-section—

chair, secretary, treasurer and other officers. As I noted in Chapter 1, my focus is on voluntary associations, political and pressure groups and community, local and social organisations, though particularly the sections on chair and secretary are more generally applicable. Then I look at the role of the 'ordinary member' in committees and larger meetings, taking a 'bottom-up' view in contrast to most of this book which in discussing how to run meetings is 'top-down': how can ordinary members influence what happens?

One effect of setting out the roles and responsibilities as I do is that they sound very heavy and complex – who's going to take this much on? But I have written about the potential range of a job and in practice any one post in any one association does not spread so far. Often the problem faced by office-holders is, surprisingly, that members are too ready not to mind if we backslide. Mike has done so many things we can't expect him to deliver the annual report on time. Stevie has spent so much time on the plans for the fortified creche that it seems unkind to point out she has forgotten the toilets. Perhaps it would be less harrowing if committees were sharper. It is easier to deliver on time if there is a feeling of compulsion. Perhaps also it would stop the active members taking on unrealistic work-loads and leaving possible volunteers out in the cold (see 5.1).

Another effect of setting out responsibilities as in the following sections is that everyone could become terribly conscientious at their job. The chair would run meetings like Superman and Clark Kent rolled into one. The secretary would have the members' total trust for efficiency and impartiality, always have papers ready on time and send every letter exactly as instructed but in better English. The treasurer would keep accounts of beauty and clarity, stay cool, pay up and hold a firm but human control over financial affairs. They would be a team . . . . The danger is they forget what they are doing it for, the politics, the purpose. All of this is a process to achieve something.

2.2 CHAIR

It is impossible to be the perfect chair – it is like being referee and skipper of the home side in the same match. The chair has two main and conflicting responsibilities:

—to ensure fair play in meetings;
—to lead the organisation to success.

So what do you do when a mere adventurist starts leading your committee into some idiocy under your very nose? Or when the fools ignore your heavy hints about what would be best for them?

You can view this impossible function with equanimity. See the open debate as the most important factor and accept that better decisions come out of it. I actually believe this, especially when I win. I think:

—that open debate is fruitful, enabling different perspectives, ideas and suggestions to be tried out;
—that the openness means that people are more likely to accept the legitimacy of the decision, to put it into effect or abide by it.

Consider also another aspect of what is usually expected of the chair:

—a responsibility for holding the organisation together and for acting as its political focus.

Thus, some chairs don't mind mayhem in debates so long as what emerges is a unified organisation and a clear agreement about what to do next.

Nonetheless within the responsibilities of the chair the conflicts of function and personal skills — 'role conflicts' in sociological terms — are real. The person who is good at running an organisation's own business meeting may not be able to stand up and lead in a battle with another organisation. She who is good at following constitutional procedure may be feeble at pulling strings behind the scene. She who is a persuasive lobbyist may find it tiresome to abide by her own committee's decisions.

The role of the chair is problematic in voluntary associations and pressure groups where it is seen as the top job in the organisation but the person who is top dog may be too dynamic to settle down and chair a meeting properly. It is useful to consider whether the chair should be chosen for ability to chair meetings rather than as a natural leader of persons.

Other versions
Sometimes the chair is the 'president' which may emphasise the

leadership function and imply a full-time post with managerial responsibilities. 'President' can also be a title given to someone who is being put back on the mantlepiece.

Some governmental agencies and other organisations set in a political framework with their own bureaucracies have 'executive chairmen'. The chair is appointed or elected to a paid post as the head of the organisation as well as chair of the executive committee or council.

The functions of chairing meetings and leading may be split. Some local councils have a chairman (often the mayor) and a leader. The latter is the one who dominates the making of policy, whereas the chair is Councillor Buggins whose turn has come at last.

Freakier and friendlier, or irredeemably suspicious, organisations may decide to to without a regular chair and to rotate the job, a fresh chair for each meeting.

I offer some points of discussion on the options later in this chapter.

The naming of chairs

The chair can be called 'Mr Chairman', 'Madame Chairman', 'Comrade Chairman', 'Madame Chairperson' and, I suppose, 'Mr Chairperson'. On grounds that 'chairman' skews the post towards men and that 'chairperson' is ugly, I have used the simpler term 'chair'. If 'Mr Chair', 'Madame Chair', 'Comrade Chair' or simply 'Chair' don't trip off the tongue, you can make up sentences including 'through the chair'.

CONDUCT OF MEETINGS

(Note: The orderly discussion of procedure is in Chapter 3.)
(I write as though there is a chair in office and present at the beginning of a meeting. This is not necessarily so. Some associations are rotating the chair, and in others the chair – and vice or deputy chair, if any – has not arrived. Then the first business is to elect a chair.)

The chair is responsible for running the meeting:

– for opening the meeting;
– for getting through the agenda (in good time);
– for giving people a chance to put their views;

– for seeing decisions are taken and agreed;
– for conducting votes on resolutions;
– for upholding the rules or constitution of the organisation.

This requires sensitivity to the mood of meetings, to judging when there has been enough discussion. It requires that the procedures are correct according to whatever form of constitution, rule-book or standing orders is in force or – in their absence – to a reasonable view of fair conduct. Two overriding points:

– the chair is neutral;
– the chair is in charge.

How the chair conducts the meeting and behaves herself depends on the kind of meeting and kind of organisation. Chairing a large, formal public meeting is very different from a business-like working party or familiar small committee. I begin by outlining the role of chair in a large, formal meeting because I think this represents an 'ideal form' of chairing from which one can relax in friendlier places.

The chair says very little. She is charged with responsibility for the procedures and progress of the meeting. First of all, she checks that the meeting has been properly called (see 3.2). Then her job is to follow the agenda, introduce items (not with a speech), select speakers, conduct votes, rule on points of order and ensure that the debate is conducted according to the rules. She says nothing except about procedure and is certainly not seen to be on anyone's side.

Like this:

We move now to Item 6, on the agenda, the motion proposed by Rev. Upp that 'The Association purchase two second-hand motorbikes'. I call on Rev. Upp to propose the motion.

There may be an agreed time-limit on speeches, or otherwise you judge that he has spoken for long enough:

I call on Rev. Upp to bring his remarks to a close.

Rev. Upp stops speaking or else you use your authority as chair to stop him (see 3.12). You proceed to call the other speakers, probably alternating those in favour of and those against the motion (see 3.6 and 5.1). When all speeches have been taken or sufficient time has been used, you call for the summing-up speech, take a vote and announce the result.

Then:

We move now to Item 7 on the agenda . . . .

And that is the limit of the chair's intervention, unless there are any breaches of the rules or standing orders or anyone raises a point of order on which the chair has to rule (see 3.11).

It is most important to retain this judicial umpiring when contentious motions are being proposed and opposed by warring factions: one thing at a time; one speaker at a time; one vote at a time; everything in proper order; and no-one but no-one speaks while the chair is speaking. The more conflict and disruption, the more formal and neutral the chairing. (Try turning it on if the meeting doesn't already trust you!)

More business-like meetings may not require such an Olympian approach. The chair can help by summarising previous decisions and drawing together the threads of debate:

So we come to Item 8. You remember that at the last meeting we agreed to pay £350 for a rocking horse from my friend Charles. Well, ...

And perhaps later:

It seems to me we have basically two issues. On the one hand there is the allegation that I am taking a kick-back but on the other that I have been led by the nose. . . .

The smaller, the friendlier and more business-like the meeting, usually the more the chair leaves the heights and joins in the discussion. But her role remains essentially that of a clarifier and conciliator rather than a protagonist for one point of view. The chair is always in a formal position in meetings because somebody should be sufficiently dissociated from the argument to be able to move on the procedure.

In a committee which is of one mind, a subcommittee or working party the chair may get involved in proposing a particular course of action, even winning over some members. I think it is wise, however, for the chair to be free to step back into the neutral, procedural function. At some time the chair ought to be able to say:

OK, we agree on ten gross of medical wipes.

And not to have everyone assume it was just because your argument was winning at that moment.

Traditionally considerable discretion is left to the chair about how she conducts a meeting. Moreover, if it should come to it, the law tends to uphold decisions of the chair where they were made fairly and reasonably, even if mistakenly.

The chair is in the driving seat of the meeting. The main areas of control are:

— formal procedure;
— getting through the business;
— selecting speakers;
— running a good show.

Formal procedure
The constitutional textbooks insist that the fundamental and maybe entire job of the chair is to have and apply a thorough knowledge of the constitution, rule-book or standing orders. All power derives from these rules, and they have to be followed. In some organisations the manipulation of the standing orders is tactically life or death – in the heyday of the student revolution in England conferences of the National Union of Students would sometimes spend perhaps a quarter of their debating time on procedural points.

In practice, in very many meetings the rules are referred to or consulted only as a last resort. Most meetings are conducted on a framework of civility, common sense and a conventional view of acceptable procedure. Moreover, many committees, especially in voluntary associations and interest groups, do not have written standing orders. They operate on these ordinary conventions, and even if they break down occasionally they manage to thrash out an agreed procedure for the incident. Life and work are possible without standing orders.

So, although the chair must follow the written rules or procedures, most of what she does will depend on more general human skills, such as tact and a sense of justice. In a friendly committee you should not be daunted from chairing because you would not know what to do when Reg Knutts-Payne shouts 'Point of order' – people are usually not so bumptious or else the meeting is relaxed enough for someone to rescue you.

Getting through the business

This means not only getting through the agenda – or perhaps exceptionally agreeing to adjourn it to hold over items to a later meeting –but doing so within a decent time. The trouble is that some people don't feel they have had a meeting unless it lasts until after the pubs have shut.

The chair may have helped the secretary prepare the agenda. She should deal with the business in that order, allowing sufficient time on each time. It is useful to begin with an idea of how long to devote to each item, or less rigorously of how far the meeting should have got after, say, an hour. It is up to the chair – unless the rules of debate specify time-limits – to decide when discussion should finish and the meeting should move on to the next item.

I find that knowing when to cut off discussion is the most difficult part of chairing, and the more interested and friendly the meeting the harder it is. How do you judge at what point Jo's bringing the discussion to life by reporting Mrs Smith's experience has tapered off into gossip?

That's why I have emphasised the apartness of the chair. She should be able to cut speakers off when others start shuffling their papers or inspecting how their fingers work.

The chair also needs to know her way round the subject that is being discussed – certainly to have read the papers for the meeting. Preferably she has thought through, or been briefed on, how the issue will be raised. Then she feels more confident about handling the debate and knows when the topic is exhausted.

Selecting speakers

The selection of who is going to speak is in theory the most powerful aspect of the job. The rule or convention is that the chair selects whoever catches her eye – by standing up, putting a hand up or indicating coolly with a ballpoint pen, whatever is appropriate for the meeting and size of room. This sounds ripe for abuse: the chair avoids catching the eye of anyone with whom she disagrees.

I think that the cunning refusal to look to the back right-hand corner is overrated, partly because it is bad tactics not to be straight. The surest way for a chair to lose the sympathy of a meeting is to be seen to be being unfair to one point of view. It maybe reveals how culturally limited I am, but I think that meetings normally react sympathetically to people obviously deprived of their rights. If there is a real pain waiting to speak, the best attack is to select him to speak. The difficulty is you may have to cut him off because he is using 'unparliamentary language' or going on too long, and then you have to judge when the mood of the meeting is flowing away from his right to speak towards its right not to listen and your right to conduct the meeting. (Let him go on too long, and the meeting becomes fed up with you too.)

What does work – and is a significant feature of the chair's power in small meetings – is to fail to encourage someone to speak. It is likely that someone at sometime wants to say something maybe a bit unpopular or different and has not quite gathered courage to raise a hand to speak or barge into the conversation. To fail to look encouragingly in their direction at the crucial moment can be decisive in whether or not they speak.

Often in committees the chair's job is less to select speakers than to decide who has spoken enough and who should be encouraged. Committee meetings may operate as conversations, except that only one person should speak at once; when there is a pause everyone jumps in. The chair helps the quieter members.

If you have any say in how the room is set out, make sure you can see and hear everyone. It is difficult seeing people behind you, in dark corners of halls and even in the back row of a small group.

Running a good show
Much more than the formalities and business rests with the chair. Whether or not the members have a good time, feel satisfied or interested, believe they achieved something, all depend to some extent on the chair.

Some features of this:

– encourage speakers to stay on the subject and not be repetitive. How you can or should do this varies. In a formal debate the standing orders may require that speakers are relevant, so the chair clearly has power to intervene if they are not.

Traditionally the chair does remind speakers of the need to be relevant and not repetitive. However, in politically sensitive meetings speakers may consider it their right to be irrelevant and to hammer home a point. Different ideologies as between speaker and chair add to the problem. The chair may be thoroughly bored by the repetition of phrases about 'oppression' but to say 'Thank you. We have got your point. Sit down' can aggravate the situation. In small meetings the chair may be able ever so sweetly to cut a speaker off (when you sense that other participants would approve);

– present material as though it is interesting and significant but without pre-empting discussion. The style and terms in which an item is introduced influence the way in which participants feel willing and free to join in discussion. The chair in committee should pick up silences or digressions in order to raise other pertinent points or lead the discussion back to the subject. It often encourages discussion to leave a remark hanging in the air – 'Of course, some would say the fair should never have taken place . . . ' – rather than 'Does anybody want to say anything?' The way in which the chair nudges the discussion backwards and forwards is real power: consider the opportunities of 'If I could just clarify the issues, I think that what Jo is getting at . . . ';

– remember that even in small meetings the chair tends to be the centre of attention. Experienced committee members keep half an eye on the chair, unless they are deliberately trying to ignore her. Thus the way in which the chair looks out of the window, flicks through her papers or files her nails has a profound effect on the involvement of other members.

A chair should look as though she welcomes all points of view. A chair's main enemy is to show her own fear or irritation.

The chair needs to know the style of the organisation and the mood of the meeting. What is the organisation *for*, and how does it work? One association has tight schedules of reporting back from subcommittees with all progress through formal resolutions – 'I move that the report of Baths Subcommittee is accepted' – after whisking through heaps of paper. Another goes 'Jill said she would look into it.'

What have the members come for? Is it to get through unpleasant affairs in the shortest possible time? Is it to meet friends and allies and thrash out a common stand? Is it to learn something to their advantage? You can be faced with some tricky mixes in voluntary and pressure groups. Some of the committee may be councillors and community or union activists who spend three or four evenings a week in meetings and would like an early night. Others may be on a night out which has meant hassles with baby-sitters and dinners-in-the-oven. Some people cope most easily with abstract business and are irritated by actual events. Some are baffled unless the discussion is about yesterday afternoon at five past three. Some only understand if they relate it to the North African desert. Your job – and it is tactics not just kindness – is to get them all (well?) to come again.

I suggest you look at the meeting and consider:

– that in your hands are their ambitions or sensitivities and your own survival;
– that, even if the meeting is in your neighbour's front room, you have been put in a formal position.

The control of a meeting is a very powerful position, and yet in principle it is to be done as if no personal power is involved.

POLITICAL LEADERSHIP

The chair can be seen only as the technical job of conducting meetings, but in most organisations the chair is expected – it is not written into the constitution – to carry wider responsibilities for leading or holding together the association or its committee. Even in the more limited role the functions of the chair can seldom be contained entirely within the actual meetings.

Several responsibilities are commonly expected of the chair:

– acting on behalf of the committee between meetings;
– reporting his committee's decisions and work to higher level committees and meetings (see 3.10);
– carrying forward the organisation, pursuing decisions made in meetings;
– resolving conflicts or clarifying issues to prepare for meetings;
– representing the organisation to the public or other bodies and campaigning.

The extent to which the chair performs these tasks depends partly on the other officers, and are affected by who else is powerful or can do them. The fact is, though some old committee hands prefer not to recognise it, that life goes on outside committees and public meetings. Events change, decisions may not be enforced exactly as agreed, new storms blow in. The chair has to respond, acting – with apologies for the mystical tone – as the embodiment of the committee.

Chair's action

Some events require urgent action by the committee before the next meeting, before even a special meeting can be called. Or sometimes the committee authorises the chair to act in this way or that depending on developments. In such cases the chair acts on behalf of the committee and reports his action for approval to the next meeting.

In a highly formalised structure the occasions and limits for chair's action may be written down in rules. Chairs of local authority subcommittees, for example, may be delegated to agree contracts according to set procedures and to approve expenditure up to £ . . . without submitting prior details to the committee. Sometimes the committee authorises the chair to negotiate and come to an agreement on its behalf – it cannot know the outcome of negotiations before they have taken place. But in many committees, particularly in associations which have no need of formal rules for every conceivable occasion, events arise on which the chair has not been guided and yet has to do something. Almost any kind of crisis can happen: a worker might appear to act with serious misconduct before disciplinary procedures have been agreed; the treasurer might abscond; a statement to the press might be essential.

On what issues and how the chair acts does require careful thought about precedents, policies or guidelines and about how the committee would have acted and will react. The amount of discretion which the chair has depends on how much he is trusted or how many votes he controls, and the chair often phones round to check what other members think. Another factor is the size of the decision. It would be more usual for the chair to take a holding action than do something irrevocable: to suspend a member of staff rather than dismiss; to freeze the bank account rather than institute legal proceedings against the treasurer; to reaffirm existing policy to the press rather than concoct a new line.

In most committee practice if the subsequent committee meeting fails to approve chair's decision, it is fairly dramatic. It may be very difficult to undo what the chair has done. Chair's action is therefore a powerful device open to devious abuse.

Carrying forward the organisation
It is not enough to have good meetings. Some has to do the work. The organisation has to be kept progressing or ticking over, and this is likely to involve the chair in some executive or political functions. The chair may be an activator or a conciliator, a penpusher or a firebrand.

Have the decisions taken at the meeting been implemented? I describe the executive functions of implementing committee decisions as the job of the secretary but in many organisations they are undertaken by the chair. There may be a difference in the way a secretary and chair would act: the secretary may be modelled on the faceless machine of the company secretary, whereas the chair may be a thoroughly political creature, assessing the effect of decisions, reckoning up votes and his measure of support. The chair may be the hustler. Consider how chairmen of school governing bodies may act as a political heavy and a sounding board for their headteachers, chivvying the administration of the local education authority.

In a political association or community group with its own staff it might be the chair who has the most regular contact with the workers. In an entirely voluntary society the chair shares out the executive functions with other officers and charms/prods/bullies them into doing their bit on time. There is enough work in being chair and checking on other people without taking on specific functions such as arranging parties and press conferences.

Often in a small association or working party the chair keeps the whole show on the road. It is not unusual for the chair to be the only person really committed to what the committee is doing. Perhaps it is his idea; perhaps he is publicly identified with it; perhaps all the other members are too busy chairing their own separate committees. Also in that people's commitment follows from finding some work to do (rather than the perpetual complaint that only the deeply committed will do anything), the chair has sometimes simply got so involved he has left the others out.

There are the more political aspects. The chair may have to

lobby even among the committee to get the committee's decisions accepted. The chair very probably has to set up the next meeting. You can believe in open debate but that's no reason not to try and win. A compromise; getting opponents to talk or work together again; giving them a hand out of entrenched positions; educating members into accepting a particular course of action; all the lobbying you can conceive. Very easily some chairs become the people you duck away from, always sliding up

> Did you hear about the plan to throw Jeremy out of the window? Wondered if you had any thoughts? (Not pausing for breath) I reckon . . . .

A consensus is born.

Most of the awkward jobs involving personal relationships land on the chair. The members expect him to tell his useless colleagues that the time has come to resign. He is in charge of getting the secretary and treasurer to bury the hatchet. He finds out why Stevie is sulking and Gerry, who was such a great ideas-man, no longer bothers to attend, and maybe persuades them to come to committee and put their cases calmly. He lines up the novice committee member to take greater responsibility. He makes the speech of thanks to the retiring member. And the other members watch, marking their mental scorecards.

Representing the association

Whatever the association does, the chair is likely to be involved.

The chair has to be able to speak as the association. There is a careful form of phrasing and conviction to be found between on the one hand reciting the wording of resolutions over and over again like an automaton and on the other hand letting loose and saying what you really feel. The chair is the leader but often leads from the centre – or as the focus – of the association rather than being out-front himself. He finds a personally acceptable way of stating collective policies – what does that do to the policies? He is often expected to negotiate or hustle, perhaps as an entrepreneur sounding out in advance what is feasible – what does that do to the committee's range of action?

How much a chair can do depends on his political base. The chair only acts – or only survives – on the approval of the association or committee. It is a question of honesty. And a question of practical politics: what is behind you – a likeminded group, a massive party majority, a delicate balance in which you were the compromise?

Some ceremonial functions fall to the chair – to show the flag at another association's meeting, to sit on a platform at a public meeting, etc. It may involve making a little speech but often just being there is enough, smiling or gritting teeth as appropriate.

Publicly the chair often seems to personify the organisation, but it is dangerous to conclude that the organisation is you. When you brush your hair in the mirror, do you see the Chair of the Tchaikovsky Crescent Tenants Association?

The line between public and personal life is uncertain. As chair you can be identified with a committee which has power over your friends, neighbours and workmates, and may be able to adjudicate on issues which affect the lives of those with whom you are drinking, eating and sleeping. All representatives face this to some extent, and some politicians do not find it a problem. The world of committee politics is often closer, however, and the chair has to limit his conversation about his members, even though he now actually knows who has not, say, paid the rent. It may be a sensitive business but some people are happy with formal or public office. They find it hard to be warm, loving human beings but they chair meetings like magic.

ALTERNATIVES

No-one can do all this. Nor generally do they have to because different organisations have found different ways of coping with the ranges of functions. In one association chairing the meetings is undemanding and the leadership role is assumed by a dominant thinker, so that the chair adopts a self-effacing, conciliatory role. In another a self-opiniated hustling chair has unflinching obedience from his committee. In another the chairing of meetings is a political conjuring act so that the chair has little choice but to act with caution between meetings. The functions and role permutate endlessly.

Two main alternative versions of the chair's role are worth noting.

Rotating chair
There is no person who stays in office as chair; a new chair is chosen for each meeting.

There are advantages. It does not build one person up as the top cat and allow him to claim to personify the association. It points out that chairing is a technical function for getting through the business of the meeting. It enables different people to acquire the skills. It means that meetings are not organised according to just one person's idea of what is appropriate business – a chair's, even unspoken, assumptions about what is useful discussion shape meetings to a surprising extent. It means that one person is not deprived from having their say'because they are in the chair every time. It may be appropriate for a group which is more concerned about the personal interaction of reaching a decision than about the decision itself. It may be appropriate for forums or meetings where it is the discussion which is all-important – perhaps the brain-storming phase of developing an association.

The disadvantages are that it lacks continuity and begs the question of who maintains progress between meetings. It under-rates the skill of chairing and the value of being familiar with a series of meetings. Unless someone or something else is a driving force, it may make it less likely that the business of the organisation and meeting will be achieved.

Nonetheless, some associations consider the office of chair as a short-term appointment for a few months or a year at most so that it does not encourage a style of personal leadership, whilst looking to the office of secretary for the longer continuity.

Splitting chair and leader
The way in which some local councils divide the jobs is illuminating. They elect a chair to conduct meetings and to perform ceremonial duties but recognise the leader of the majority party as the dominating and longer-lasting force. This splits the two sets of functions along the lines I have described in this chapter and avoids some of the conflicts.

The person responsible for a policy or action is not then put in the position of chairing a meeting where it is criticised, as, for example, some union presidents and company chairmen are. The opposition can see the chair as neutral rather than the enemy who is rigging the meeting against them. The leader is free from the constraints of chairing to justify himself. (There is another solution: someone else can take the chair for a particular item.)

Consider how the Prime Minister chairs the Cabinet but the Speaker (who has evolved into a largely silent creature) chairs the

House of Commons. Select Committees are chaired by MPs who are sometimes synonymous with their committees. It depends what you are trying to achieve, and in the context of the British Parliament whether it is business or debating, executive or legislative aims.

There are advantages in the traditional chair:

— to have a committee chaired by the person who will bear responsibility for implementing decisions can add authority to the chairing and immediacy to the debate — 'Look, I have to go away and do it. . . .';
— to have the leader bound to the committee as its chair is actually or potentially democratic.

2.3 SECRETARY

The secretary is the machine. He is the person who cares that constitutional procedures are followed, that notices of meetings are sent out on time, that reports are sent in on time and that the organisation conforms, on the whole, to the law. The secretary is responsible for the preparation of meetings, for administration and for progress-chasing.

In committees which are backed up by full-time staff there are different versions of being secretary:

— the self-effacing clerk who only speaks when spoken to, who handles the paperwork of sending out notices and reports and who during the meeting keeps his head down taking the minutes;
— the chief executive of the organisation or the head of its administrative and financial side, like the 'company secretary', who is the connection between the committee and the staff, and who therefore speaks up in committee for reality, for expert knowledge and for getting things done;
— a member rather than an employee (as the two previous versions are) who doesn't personally do the secretary's work but sees that the staff do, again connecting the strange band of politicians, busy-bodies and Methodist clergy who sit on the committee with the dedicated professionals who form the staff;
— a member who voluntarily does the committee-work side of the

secretary's job so that a small staff can get on with the real work
of the association, running a playground, social club, youth
centre etc.

The clerk of a school governing body, the general secretary of a
trade union, a company secretary all act as secretaries though the
weight they carry in their committees and their organisations
varies greatly. They are all servants of their committees, responsible for seeing that the committee functions properly and
that its instructions are carried out.

In a voluntary group the secretary covers all these functions, and if he occasionally looks harassed that is only what
other members of committee expect. During a meeting he may
have to concentrate on taking minutes and noting who does what,
he may be fretting that Positive Experiences Subcommittee has
failed yet again to produce a report and he is worrying whether he
can buy big enough envelopes to send members, as just decided,
the consultative document on *The local community in the post-
technological age: A draft proposal for retooling the personal and
social infrastructure.* He sits behind a heap of neat documen-
tation, pen and notebook at the ready, teeth grinding, though
quietly so as not to indicate any disloyalty to the chair. Yet he may
know more about what happens outside the meeting than anyone
else and has actually read the papers for the meeting, unlike the
self-appointed 'people's advocate' who is speaking at present. He
may be the person who more than any other has kept the
association running for the past few years, chivvying members to
do what they had promised, filling the gaps, meeting deputations,
turning up at meetings even when the European Cup Final was on
television. Is he really expected to sit there through this?

Yes. But see how a powerful secretary *serves* his committee. Of
course, he presents papers and issues fairly and carries out
instructions. But he has chatted to the person who is writing the
paper 'merely' to fill in the background, set out some of the
constraints and indicate how the committee usually finds it
helpful to tackle issues

To me, Stevie, it's neither here nor there whether the meeting
decides to barricade the windows at once (*or* Personally, I'm
right with you on the need for firm action . . .), but remember-
ing the way the members reacted to your subcommittee's idea

for taking over the council chamber as a creche, I wonder whether we shouldn't give them a let-out so you can get their commitment to the principle and get them to agree to sending a deputation. Then, if nothing comes of that we can go back to the next meeting with this tough line. The danger for you, as I read it, is that the committee will simply shoot down out of hand the proposal for armour-plating the front door – they'll be worried about the landlord and the implications for the insurance policy and so on – and we'll just be back in the old confrontation era all over again.

In committee he keeps clarifying discussions until they turn into what he sees as a viable decision

Can I check back, Mr Chairman, that we were suggesting that the team should be chosen by some kind of selection committee. . . .
And the idea was that. . . .
So if I just tidy this up for the minutes. . . .

The secretary is often better placed than the chair to *guide* decisions. If the chair is unfair to one faction or heaves the committee round to a different direction, it tends to show up in public. The secretary, however, looks after the material which is presented to committee and the instructions which it issues. He is meant to be concerned that the committee is given information which it can handle and that it comes to decisions which it can have put into effect. Thus, much of his influence is before and after the meeting, and even during the meeting he works as clarifier and practical man, rather than arguing for one point of view. A secretary can be a puppet-master in much the same way as senior civil servants can pull the strings on their political masters.

BEFORE THE MEETING

The secretary is responsible for preparing everything for the meeting. Whereas other members can just turn up on the day, the secretary has to start thinking about a meeting some days or weeks before.

Notice of meetings
(See 3.2)

The secretary has to send out the notice which tells everyone, who is entitled to attend, that the meeting is to take place, where and when. It should say in the constitution how many days notice is required, whether a fortnight, five clear days, two working days etc. If not, the secretary has to decide how much notice people need – to be fair and to make sure of a good attendance. Unless it is an emergency, less than a week or a fortnight is impossible, and if people are not expecting the meeting, you should give longer.

Some meetings can be demanded by members. The constitution says something like

> A special general meeting of the association may be requested by not less than twelve members, and upon receiving such a request the secretary shall take all necessary steps to call such a meeting within three weeks.

In calling the meetings the secretary has to be efficient and fair. It is a dreadful nuisance having to remember that the executive committee meets in a fortnight, and in a small association it means typing, duplicating, stuffing envelopes and buying stamps yourself, but it just has to be done.

Likewise, it is tempting when the usual trouble-makers request a special meeting to see if you can't say that their letter must have got lost in the post or if you can't hang on a bit. But, apart from the dishonesty and that in itself undermines the association, I think such tactics are likely to be self-defeating. The demand for a special meeting shows some loss of confidence in the way the association is running, and if the secretary does not respond impartially he aggravates the situation. The 'trouble-makers' build up more steam and create more trouble. I suppose you might succeed in bottling them up or in driving them away in disgust. But the secretary must

– play by the rules, and/or
– be confident that his point of view will win, and/or
– recognise that associations need some dissent and different arguments.

In this the secretary has to see himself as just a machine for processing the notices of meetings, for carrying out what the rules require.

Agenda
(See 3.3)
The agenda is normally sent out with the notice of the meeting. It lists in order what items are to be discussed at the meeting.

Secretaries often consult the chair and other members of committee about what should go on the agenda. Sometimes they ask members to drop them a note of what items they want raised. As I point out in Chapter 3.3, what goes on the agenda is politically crucial, and in some elaborate associations it is so sensitive that a small committee has to be formed to draw up the agenda.

Drawing up the agenda depends on

— knowing what is happening in the association,
— knowing what decisions are needed at this time, and
— thinking about the most effective order to take items.

Remember that the meeting can only discuss what is on the agenda. (Although 'Any other business' at the end of the agenda can provide an escape for things forgotten or urgent, a sharp chair would not allow major issues to be raised here.) So the secretary needs to be aware whether in the outlying reaches of the association things are bubbling up which ought to be raised in committee. Is the gossip about corruption in the table tennis competition strong enough or substantial enough that the committee ought to be prompted to sort it out? Will members want to discuss the impact of the Government's policies?

The secretary must be aware of what decisions are due, perhaps keeping a checklist or a file. Was Bar Subcommittee instructed by the Executive Committee to report on prices to this meeting? If a change to the constitution requires (according to the constitution) four weeks notice to executive members and then two weeks notice to the AGM, is there time to set up a working party to consider the issues or will the recommendation have to be made at this meeting? Surely, the treasurer should be able to report the figures for expenditure by now? Has Mrs Mackay time to make the Christmas puddings, if the bazaar is not put on the agenda for

October? Is the debate about the principle of admission fees more urgent than the decision on hiring a minibus?

Some things the secretary would prefer not to have discussed. He thinks they will be destructive or he thinks his side, if he has one, will lose. To put the break-in at the youth centre down as a separate item on the agenda (rather than mentioning it in passing in the chair's report) will give Stevie the opportunity to complain about the local police again, and that will infuriate the representatives from the Residents' Association, and the anger will carry over and scupper the fund-raising fete. If we discuss the Government's policy now right after the budget, the left-wing will be supported by the wishy-washy liberals. Dare we talk about the darts league in relation to ethnic minorities? Will Geoff be mortally offended by a full-blown discussion on the cleaning? Is a debate about salaries going to lead to a motion of 'No confidence' in the negotiating committee?

In these political judgements the secretary's job is a little easier in the more formal, traditional kind of meeting where the agenda comprises reports from officers and subcommittees and motions. It is strictly speaking up to the subcommittee or officer what it reports, and all motions which are properly submitted must be debated. If Maintenance Subcommittee's report or minutes includes criticism of the cleaning or if a motion is submitted, duly proposed and seconded, according to the rules,

> That the cleaning of the hall is inadequate and the following measures be taken . . . . ,

the secretary, machine-like, puts them on the agenda.

But many committees and meetings work, at least partly, through discussions on topics, and then the secretary has to decide which topics are important and timely. He may talk it over with the chair and the most powerful members. The secretary should consider:

- that open discussion is part of the rationale for the whole · process of committees and meetings;
- that putting the lid on problems can be more explosive than dealing with them earlier, perhaps obliquely;
- that, on the other hand, some problems do disappear spontaneously;

— that uninformed, unstructured discussion is more likely to be destructive than a discussion where you, the chair or another member is well-briefed and has thought through how the debate will develop and what can be proposed at the end.

Suppose, the absence of people from ethnic minorities in the darts league has become 'an issue', and the secretary recognises it is a nasty and difficult topic for his committee to discuss. Can he hope that it is reckoned to be outside his committee's scope? Will it go away by itself? What good can come of pretending it is not happening? And is there a risk that if it is not on the agenda a member will raise it under Sports Subcommittee's report when you're off-guard? Are you wishing that six months ago you had intervened, had a quiet word with the organisers or formed a multi-racial team? You decide to put it on the agenda

    6. Darts league — involvement of ethnic minorities.

I think you would be wrong to introduce it:

I've heard that it is difficult for people from ethnic minorities to get into the darts league. Has anyone heard anything? Got anything to say?

This approach most likely produces:

Well, when I popped into the Bull and Artist I noticed. . . .
Of course, they don't actually want to play darts. . . .
It's just . . . stirring things up. . . .
What do you know about what they want. . . .

Moral indignation all round; few facts but plenty of emotive outbursts; entrenchment of positions and no direction to the discussion; either no decision or one that is patched up on the spot and unlikely to hold together after the meeting.

    Far better, I think, to set up someone to present a verbal, or even written, report which sets out facts, issues, the law (if relevant) and which is based on contact with the various sides in such a dispute. What is the situation? What would different parties like to happen to resolve it? Such information and structure makes it more likely that you will get a workable decision, though, of course, it does not guarantee anything. The secretary has to think of this in drawing up the agenda and get it ready for the meeting.

For everyone running a committee or meeting a major problem is how to lead it into making a decision. The secretary's work on the agenda contributes to this. He has selected, as discussed, the right items and has prepared the ground for them. He should also have a clear view of the status of different discussions. Must the committee make a decision? Or, is this just for information? If a decision is required will it be formed from the recommendations of a subcommittee or officer, or from a motion, proposed, debated and resolved? If it is information, is it contentious, interesting or merely routine? Alternatively, this committee may not be entitled to authorise such action: it may only be able to make a recommendation to a superior meeting (see 3.1). You can note the status on the agenda

7. Youth centre – break-in FOR INFORMATION
8. Summer fete
    TO RECEIVE A REPORT FROM FETE WORKING PARTY AND TO APPROVE ITS RECOMMEN-DATIONS
9. Government finance for community projects (*Investment in initiative*)
    TO RECEIVE A REPORT FROM THE VICE-CHAIR (EXTERNAL RELATIONS) AND TO AGREE RE-COMMENDATIONS TO PUT TO THE GENERAL MEETING.

You may find the formality and discipline off-putting and bureaucratic. At least, know in your own mind how the process fits together so you can push and pull the meeting into deciding the right kind of action.

I discuss the order of agenda items in Chapter 3.3.

Committee papers
With the agenda come the written reports from officers and working parties and the minutes or reports from subcommittees, though some committees stay free of this much paper. The secretary makes sure that either these papers are sent out with the agenda or that they are ready on the table at the meeting.

This is straightforward. You are immaculately efficient and chase people ruthlessly to deliver on time in your own inimitable way.

The secretary keeps his eye on what other papers and information would help the meeting come to a decision, as in the example above:

— facts and figures;
— analysis of the issues;
— the legal implications;
— the financial implications, unless this is a treasurer's responsibility;
— existing policies and precedents on this topic.

Constitutional changes

It is usually to the secretary that any changes to the constitution must be submitted. Again, the secretary processes these according to the rules in the constitution. He may offer advice about wording such changes but he does not normally have any discretion. He receives the proposal, puts it on the relevant agenda and circulates it as required.

Setting up the meeting

The secretary probably has to book the room or hall for a meeting – it looks very silly if you forget. You, if anyone, are the person who sets up the room, the chairs, perhaps a jug of water for the chair and speaker, blackboards, charts etc.

Likewise, it is the secretary who invites speakers and guests, as instructed by the meeting.

IN THE MEETING

Minutes

(See 3.4)

Some associations have a separate minutes secretary, a dormouse with perfect shorthand, thus freeing the secretary to take a more active part in meetings. Taking minutes means having pen and paper at the ready to note:

— the main points of discussions;

- the wording of resolutions and other decisions, including the person or body which is instructed to act;
- the outcome of votes;
- the names of speakers (even if you don't write them into the minutes, it helps recall what happened when you come to write them up);
- in debates of motions and amendments, the wording of all motions and amendments proposed with the name of the proposer and, if appropriate, seconder;
- in elections, the names of all candidates with their proposers (and seconders) and the voting figures.

It means you are less able to contribute to the discussion. Joining in is frowned upon in some meetings; it does make people wonder about the impartiality of the minutes if the secretary has spoken passionately.

With formal motions and amendments the secretary must be absolutely sure of the wording (interrupt the meeting to check if necessary) but has a relatively automatic task of writing them up. More problematic are those rambling committee discussions where the chair hears a silence and announces

Well, we've approved that

and leaves the secretary to sort it out. Just in time to get the minutes out for the next meeting you look at your pages of scribble . . . . It would have been better to have asked at the time

Can I check for the minutes exactly what we have decided.

It's also good for the meeting because probably they too are confused.

Simple minutes, if you are familiar with the committee, can be written up as you go through the meeting. More often, secretaries take notes and write them up later, maybe consulting with the chair. (If he disagrees with the chair, he should stick to his own interpretation.)

There are different styles of minutes, as I illustrate in Chapter 3.4. They are always records of the decisions, usually records of the main points of discussion and argument, sometimes an exposition of the issues, occasionally detailed reporting of speeches. They are not commentaries or imaginative reconstructions.

It seems like drudgery and maybe stops you saying what you think. However, it is:

- an opportunity to work yourself into an organisation;
- personally satisfying to sort out a discussion into some sharp minutes that make sense of what happened;
- a chance to shape the way the association thinks about issues, not by outright bias but by using one form of words rather than another, by recording, say, the constructive rather than the extreme and controversial arguments, or vice versa.

You are creating the association's memory.

The next meeting begins by checking the minutes of the previous meeting for accuracy. Usually the secretary has typed, duplicated and circulated them before the meeting but sometimes he reads them from a handwritten minutes book. He should try and not think that corrections to the minutes are a personal insult to his shorthand/integrity/memory: disentangling a meeting is complex. Equally, he should resist attempts to have minutes 'corrected' to what some members wish they had decided. Once the minutes have been confirmed by the meeting and signed by the chair, they are the authoritative, constitutional record of what happened.

The secretary keeps the minutes on file or in a bound minutes book, together with the agenda, reports and papers submitted to the meeting.

Correspondence
(See 3.3)
In some associations the secretary reports to the meetings all or major correspondence received. He may have channelled contentious issues into separate items on the agenda.

The meeting instructs the secretary how to react

Petition from the 4th XI about the state of the equipment – Thank them for bringing it to the attention of the committee and point out the shortage of funds. Leaflet from publishers about a new book on running committees – Order two copies from the bookseller. Letter from solicitors about new legislation – Investigate and report to the next meeting.

The secretary carries out these instructions.

Elections
(See 3.9)
The secretary may be responsible for running elections, often because his post is separate from the rest of the committee (see below). The constitution describes how the proposals must be submitted, and there may be rules about the conduct of elections by post or in the meeting. The secretary circulates a notice calling for nominations to be sent in to him, or whatever the rules say. The secretary plays it exactly by the book and wears a mask of neutrality. He hasn't lost the fascists' voting forms; he doesn't grimace when his enemies are proposed for office; he counts the votes accurately.

Voluntary groups often need to cajole people to stand for office. The secretary should know how generous and persuasive to be. It's quite common for, say, eight names put up for six or seven places and the AGM decide to elect them all or to have the extra one or two appointed as coopted members. Where everyone is friendly it is hard to resist this at the time, but later if votes in the committee become critical you can live to regret such big-heartedness. In a friendly and secure organisation the secretary leads the outgoing committee either to arrange for the right number of nominations to fill the posts or to collect so many names that those who lose do not feel terribly insulted. Egos crack easily during elections – next year it may be yours.

Some large, politically high-powered associations have separate elections officers or subcommittees or call in the Electoral Reform Society.

AFTER THE MEETING

Clearing up
If it was you who set up the chairs and the water jug, it is you who clears them away.

Are you expected to write a letter of thanks to the owner of the room and any speakers or visiting experts?

Carrying out instructions
It is during the following weeks that you are glad you took such a good note of who was instructed to do what

> Yes, Stevie, I've got it written in my note-book (and that's what's appearing in the minutes) and *you* were going to look into anti-vandal paint and produce a report.
> No, Hon. Treasurer, you can only spend up to £50 on publicity for the fete.
> You volunteered . . . .
> The executive authorised you to sign a cheque for £37.80 for sports gear. Here it is.
> The committee decided to have a public meeting and, even if you don't think it's a good idea, the committee said . . . .

He does what he was instructed to do, coordinates the committee and, if there are staff, may be the link between the politicians and the administrators. These jobs are likely to be shared with the chair, in which case the secretary is likely to take the committee business, procedural matters and correspondence while the chair handles more public and political business.

WIDER ROLES

Legal and constitutional responsibilities
In some organisations the secretary has duties which are prescribed by law or by the regulations under which they operate. If we were approaching the functions of the secretary from the point of view of a company secretary, we would need to begin with her legal responsibilities. A voluntary pressure group may also find it useful to look briefly at such legal duties, even though they do not technically apply, to fill out the secretary's area of responsibility.

The secretary of a company has duties described in the Companies Acts. She is responsible for keeping the Statutory Books, keeping records of shares, submitting annual accounts and reports and delivering registration documents to the Registrar of Companies. A company secretary can be held personally responsible for performing these duties and can – though in practice it is not likely if she has acted in good faith – be fined for failing to do so. The secretary is not just a member of the board of directors with added burdens: the secretary is an

employee, appointed by the board, but has like members of the
board legal duties.   ·

On this model some kinds of associations put legal responsibilities upon the person of the secretary. The secretary
is appointed not as one of the committee but separately as an officer with her own status. The secretary of a housing society, for
example, is not just one of the elected committee who happens to
look after the correspondence, minutes, agenda and so forth, but
has duties described in the society's rules. She is appointed by the
AGM or the management committee and may even not be one of
their members but an agent employed to perform these duties.
The secretary is the official channel of communication between
the society and superior bodies or Government agencies (in the
case of a housing society, the Housing Corporation).

In an organisation which works on principles similar to
registered companies the secretary is also responsible for the
accounts and financial business of the organisation. She may have
prescribed legal responsibilities to see that annual accounts are
audited and returned to the appropriate body and perhaps that
annual reports, constitutional changes and lists of members are
submitted.

The constitution or rules of an organisation probably give the
secretary the duties of calling meetings and of elections, and the
secretary has similar impartial duties in presenting minutes and
processing constitutional changes. Thus, the secretary is a
constitutional conscience on a committee, knowing what the
constitution allows to be done and reminding the committee of
precedents and previous resolutions on the subject. It is true that
it is the chair's responsibility to rule on the constitution during a
meeting, if necessary, but nonetheless the secretary is briefed on
constitutional implications and regards it as her duty to spell
them out if occasion arises.

Administrative functions
The secretary is responsible for incoming and outgoing correspondence and is conventionally the officer who keeps the organisation running. If there are paid workers or a whole bureaucracy,
she coordinates between them and the committee. In a small
group the secretary is the person who – voluntarily – runs the
office, though the office does only consist of an address for
receiving mail and a ragged box-file. In some longer-lasting

pressure groups it has been the secretary who has served year after year and held the outfit together, rather than chairs and other members who have come and gone as personal whim and the will of the electorate took them. The secretary has devoted many hours or even days a week to the job, given over the spare room or the toolshed to the files, the information banks and the back-copies of the newsletter and has personified the association.

The role is further developed in the general secretary of a trade union, elected to a full-time post and the head of the administration. The general secretary, though answerable to an executive, is often effectively the leader of the organisation. The media and thereby the public see them as the boss of a union, even if technically they are the officer of an executive committee.

The secretaryship of a voluntary organisation is a job for someone who is industrious, who can find things in files, is – or looks – impartial. She may well hold the crucial position between a fly chair and miserly treasurer, or she may provide the backroom effort for a politically powerful chair. She may type and lick envelopes or appear to the outside world as though it is she who runs the association.

2.4 TREASURER

The treasurer is the boring one who chirps up about not being able to afford things, about budgets and authorisations for expenditure. OK, so he has got his bookkeeping system to think about, but why he won't let me deduct the money for the postage stamps from the memberships subscriptions, I fail to understand. . . . And really unless I can keep a bit of cash around, just £30 in a tin box/£300 in the safe, I spend all my time in the bank, which is never open anyway. . . . Back in May he said he'd allocated £12.50/£7,800 to pay for the conference, and now we're not having the conference it would seem only sensible as the money is there to spend it on a really big, impressive edition of *What we think*, but 'Oh no, not him' . . . . I could have sold the committee my mother's old dining room chairs and we could have saved £150 but she needed the cash then, not after three weeks and another wretched committee meeting. . . . I know I forgot to pick up a chit, but for 78p/£32.53 I'd almost rather pay it myself than go through all this fuss. . . . Doesn't he trust us?

Good treasurers are had to come by. Perhaps it is because the rest of the world goes on as above. There ought not to be anything to be ashamed of in being able to look after money, and actually the qualities that most associations need in a treasurer are not peculiar:

- ordinary honesty;
- ability to keep straight, clear records and accounts;
- familiarity with money at the level with which the association deals, whether pence or thousands of pounds;
- skill and conscience about financial propriety and viability;
- commitment to the same purposes as the rest of the association.

These qualities need not, as far as many associations are concerned, be at an elevated expert level. I suspect that often we look for financial geniuses or even chartered accountants when someone who could manage their own housekeeping properly would be adequate.

But somehow the person who is good at controlling the cash begins to resent paying it out, or at least it seems so and that creates resentment. Sometimes, in complete contrast, they get ashamed of being obsessed with money and become amiable and glad-handed. The perfect person is in such demand by other associations that she is too busy to come to the meetings. The financial wizard frightens the other members by her casualness over 35p/£350.

The treasurer's job is in some ways a lonely and difficult position in a committee. First, the treasurer is usually expected to have a responsibility to the whole membership in a more rigorous way than, perhaps, the other members do. Once elected, the chair and secretary may feel, and other members almost certainly will feel, that they are free or mandated to pursue their policies. But the treasurer is usually thought to have a wider responsibility than just to the winning majority of the electorate: to public standards of propriety, including in some bodies personal responsibility to a public watchdog; to the trustees, if any; to the whole membership or contributors of funds. Thus, the treasurer is sometimes put in the position of arguing an objective, conscientious or legal case against the political will of the committee.

A second area of difficulty follows from this. Because it is recognised that she has a public or wider responsibility like this, when she speaks on financial matters it is taken that she has considerable clout, that she is not to be overruled or opposed at all lightly. The treasurer warns: 'This proposal for expenditure may be ultra vires' or 'The funds are not available to do this'. We've got to believe it. Then, we should expect of the treasurer not only financial integrity but political integrity. Another member of the executive tells the meeting: 'It's all very well having these radical fantasies but how, I ask you, are you going to pay for them? There is no money in the bank'. The treasurer intervenes with a 'point of information' or speaks later: 'If the motion is passed, we could allocate these funds . . .'. Unfortunately the requirement to account for expenditure tempts treasurers find it easier to channel funds into established rather than radical activities. Worse, they are quite commonly put up by ruling groups on committees as the last ditch defence. ('If we can't win them over by argument, we'll tell them there's no money for it. Unless they like to make a voluntary contribution themselves. That'll sort'em out.') Conversely, it is true that meetings quite commonly have more ideas about good things than about paying for them. An excellent treasurer has to examine conscientiously not only the accounts but her own judgment.

But, once a decision has been made, the treasurer does have to pay out on what has been constitutionally agreed. That must be an aspect of her responsibility to the association. She does not continue to obstruct what she wishes had not been agreed or keep finding technical difficulties. ('Alright, so it's not really ultra vires, but I don't quite see which head of expenditure I can put it under. When I've resolved that problem I'll get the forms printed and consult with the chairman on the procedures for authorisation. In five or six weeks I should have it sorted out, perhaps') The treasurer should remember that orderly finances are seldom the main purpose of an association; she is there to facilitate activities.

Like other elected members, at some time she may receive a constitutional or legitimate instruction which is abhorrent, and the treasurer makes the political and moral choice of whether to implement it as she should, to honourably resign or not to implement it and pray that history at least will smile on her. In some associations this choice lands on the treasurer more often than most.

In some associations the post of treasurer is a special one to which someone not involved in the hurly-burly is appointed or elected. Or it may be just one post among others which the management committee divides up among its members. It is anyway common to treat it as a longer-term commitment than the comings-and-goings of other officers, particularly when a treasurer does manage to establish herself as 'above politics'. It takes time to understand even a small association's finances and to sort out how to control them.

IN MEETINGS

The treasurer

– presents financial reports and accounts,
– submits estimates of expenditure for approval, and
– comments on proposals for their financial feasibility and propriety.

The treasurer may have a regular item on the agenda for a report of income and expenditure or may present these accounts quarterly. Some associations only receive accounts from their treasurer once a year when he presents the annual accounts for approval, though this suggests that either the association is very lax or has very little financial business. The accounts should be presented on paper, sent out to members with time enough for them to read them and should be explained verbally by the treasurer at the meeting. Often the other members just see a blur of figures, left-hand columns and right-hand columns that somehow come to the same total and approve them on the nod. Sometimes a member blows the whistle: 'What's this about £36 for publicity? I don't remember any publicity.'

To get a committee to talk about the main issues involved requires, unless it is an expert committee, a long process of education by the treasurer. Treasurers have been known to have mixed feelings about this. If he makes the accounts clear – as undoubtedly he should – it is easier for people to argue with them, whereas if he whisks them past the committee's nose most committees will not challenge him. People tend to believe figures written on paper.

Annual accounts
Annual accounts are usually presented in draft form to the

executive or management committee, sent to accountants for auditing and then presented as final, audited accounts for approval at the annual general meeting. The approval of the annual accounts is a main function of the AGM. The constitution also often has the AGM select the auditors for the following year's accounts. Considering the importance which the law and various public watchdogs attach to the financial affairs of associations (see Chapter 4), it is surprising how casual AGMs are about annual accounts. The accounts are not ready yet, but perhaps you would like to see a draft now and authorise the executive to approve them later. The previous treasurer has not yet handed over the books. I'm afraid I've had a terrible time at work and haven't managed it yet. Or else

Chair: I call on the treasurer to present the annual accounts.
Treasurer: I have circulated copies of the audited accounts. Could I formally move their adoption, Mr. Chair.
Chair: Is that agreed?
Everyone: Yes/OK/Aye.

The treasurer thinks both 'That's a relief' and 'After all my hard work the layabout don't give a damn'.

Members may need to be persuaded that the annual accounts are not merely uninteresting sums about money which has been spent already but are a record of how effectively the association has been carrying out its activities.

Estimates

The treasurer before the beginning of the association's financial year draws up estimates of income and expenditure for the coming year. One way, very crudely, is to take the previous year's estimates, look at how expenditure is actually turning out, adjust those estimates accordingly and add on a percentage for inflation. That way you provide for doing the same activities year after year. So long as you remember to take the decision to increase your income at the same rate as inflation is increasing your expenditure. The other way is to review all your activities in the light of current policies, estimate how much they will cost, evaluate which the association regards as essential and which optional, see how they match up to likely income and then start cutting expenditure and increasing income until the two columns are the same. (Either way, you include some form of contingency fund for unforeseen expenditure, mistakes in calculations, additional inflation etc.) Even this ridiculously crude summary of what some people give their lives to (and others do on the back of an envelope) shows that policy decisions are involved. Thus the treasurer may need to lead the committee into a review of the association's activities. The committee, however, is all too likely to regard the estimates as a mere technical job which the treasurer does by himself (or with whatever financial staff the association has), but the effect is that basic establishment costs continue to increase and the amount of money available for activities gets proportionately smaller year-by-year.

Miracles

The treasurer sits through the meeting watching for anything which involves income or expenditure. He is ready to discuss the feasibility of projects; indeed, before the meeting he has anticipated what issues will arise. He warns about any principles which are involved. He works out at amazing speed where the money can come from, juggling with accounting heads, slipping money this way and that to match the decisions. He retains enough cool to know when to recommend further consideration of an item or an instruction to himself (or his subcommittee) to produce the figures for the next meeting. He knows that the meeting expects him to intervene on any financial matters and therefore does so confidently. He never puts his head down and thinks 'Just let them go ahead and see what mess they get into'. He is a saint, and the people love him.

THE ORGANISATION

The treasurer is often seen as controlling and keeping records of all aspects of income and expenditure, as well as being the expert on any other financial matters which crop up from insurance policies to rents. But actually when we think about a particular association we find that various other functions of raising and spending money are performed by other people. The membership secretary collects subscriptions; the publications secretary pays for journals; the secretary buys stationery; or, on a larger scale, the chief officer authorises a whole range of expenditure. So a prime function of the treasurer is to sort out who is responsible for what and how they conduct business between themselves. If, say, there is a vice-president (finance), how do those responsibilities relate to the treasurer's? What expenditure can the chair of a subcommittee which organises a dance authorise? What records are kept when the membership secretary hands over a subscription? When the secretary is asked to sign a cheque, what evidence is provided of what it is for? What are the limits on an officers powers of expenditure – £500, £50 or what's left in the petty cash box?

Controls

This is not the place to advise on how to keep accounts or be an accountant (see Further Reading), but there are some principles which closely relate to this book's discussion of structures and procedures in committees and meetings.

A committee or meeting needs to know that definitions of responsibility and control mechanisms have been established and are being followed. I suggest these mechanisms must be:

– clear enough that anyone can tell whose job is which (Never: I thought he was meant to do that, not me.);
– simple enough that people never have the excuse they were too much bother;
– appropriate so that they help the association achieve its aims.

If they do not already exist, the treasurer devises the definitions of responsibility and control mechanisms and puts them to the meeting for approval. Once agreed, they are followed unswervingly.

Two objections are raised to strict agreed procedures. First, that the association wants to involve many people and cannot bog them down in the paperwork. Membership subscriptions are collected by people with responsibility for their own patch and they simply ignore cumbersome instructions. I think this is right but ought to be seen as an argument for a simple system with a straightforward record of each transaction from one person to another – a signature on a record card or book, a petty cash form, etc.

Secondly, that we are all friends, trust each other and could be flexible. This, too, could be right – except that in a voluntary association the effects of mere suspicion can be ruinous, let alone of finding someone with their hand in the till. One purpose of the procedures is to show publicly that it is very difficult and un- likely that the treasurer is planning a trip to Bali on our funds. People even wince when they pay their subscription and see the membership secretary buy a drink with the same £1 note later that evening. Honesty should be seen to be done. If we get to demanding an investigation, much of the damage is done.

So for the committee the fact that other people than the treasurer are involved is not an inconvenience. It is one of the ways in which the control of income and expenditure is made open. It is not just one person who is liable to be tempted or hoodwinked or who slips up in their addition. We know that the income is checked. We know that payments are authorised by agreed people or committees to meet expenditures which have been properly approved.

For similar reasons the funds are kept in a bank account in the association's name (i.e. separate from our own money); income does not hang around but is banked; and cheques require two signatures.

The end of this process of checking is when at the end of the year the accounts, books and financial records, chits for payment etc. are submitted to independent accountants for auditing.

Monitoring

The committee also requires accounts so that it can monitor income and expenditure. We don't wish to discover in November that the money is all gone, nor at the end of the year that there is a surplus which could have been spent earlier. The monitoring is achieved by the regular or quarterly accounts but it should be possible also, given some notice, to check easily on spending on all or some activities. The treasurer therefore needs a system which, at its simplest by reference to her cashbook, will provide this information.

The treasurer should remember the personal stake in the finances of a voluntary association. Maybe in a commercial undertaking the buck stops in the vast reserves of the International Multinational Amalgamated Neighbourhood Bank, but in voluntary associations we as individuals are very often liable (see Chapter 4). We cannot afford to let the treasurer forget that the committee relies on her controls.

2.5 OTHER OFFICERS

Membership secretary, social secretary, publicity officer, newsletter editor, publications officer, complaints officer, political education officer, fixtures secretary, 1st XI captain, wine secretary. Or, a system of subcommittees with their chairs: chair of membership subcommittee, chair of social subcommittee. Or, various deputy and vice-chairs and presidents: deputy chair (publicity), vice-president (complaints), vice-chair (games). It depends what the association does.

Some posts may be required by the constitution, but constitutions frequently state broadly '. . . and such other officers as the committee may from time to time decide'. So posts may be created as needed – and lapsed when the need is over. Giving people fancy titles is a way of getting them to do some work: 'If we make him vice-chair (external relations), perhaps we can get him to go and talk to someone.' But usually a committee has a fairly constant sets of posts according to its main functions.

What criteria are there for creating posts? Primarily that the committee has an important task which can be allocated to one person (or subcommittee). You don't set up a post for something which isn't fairly significant but equally you don't for the whole function of the association. But then there are two conflicting criteria:

– it is useful to spread these posts around as a means of involving people;
– it is silly to multiply posts and create a byzantine court of vice-chairs for this and that, secretaries for collecting the tea-money and buying the biscuits, and worse, when Biscuits Secretary has an off-day disaster ensues because no-one else knows the system.

The creation of posts should be matched to the tasks which the association needs performed and to people's skills (see 5.1). There may be no point in having a publicity officer if nobody is up to the job and if anyway the chair can do it easily. But, conversely, even if no-one enjoys collecting membership subscriptions, the association may find it absolutely essential that someone takes this responsibility. There may be ways of dividing up responsibilities differently. The cricket club (probably) has to have a 1st XI captain, but although when Sammy was skipper he organised the groundman, the transport for 'away' matches and the beer kitty, to fit other people's skills you could have a transport secretary or a grounds secretary and make the twelfth man fetch the beer. For our own association, come the annual general meeting or the first meeting of the new executive, we tend automatically to fill the same posts as last year.

IN THE MEETING

As with the treasurer, the officer with a particular responsibility reports to and takes instructions from the meetings, whilst watching for issues and items which relate to her responsibility. She – as I suggested for the treasurer – should report clearly and regularly, making the functions open to the rest of the committee. She may need to submit an annual report and perhaps a plan for a range of future activities. She needs to be clear how much authority she has to act and at which points she should get the approval of the committee in advance. The membership secretary requires prior approval from the committee to raise subscriptions but may have discretion about how they are collected. The publicity officer may need to submit a written press statement for approval but has discretion in talking on the phone to the press.

These posts are not mostly such specialist functions as the treasurer; nor do they have that sacred higher duty. They all are expected to join in discussions as committee member rather than only as a particular functionary. If the publicity officer only speaks about publicity and the political education officer only speaks about the hearts and minds of the people, there is no general debate at all. Everybody says 'Oh, Winston is the expert on publicity, so we'll agree with whatever he says' and then 'Nigel is in charge of telling people what's good for them, so we'll go along with him'. You just get mutual flattery, everyone with their own empire.

IN THE WORK OF THE ASSOCIATION

We have to be able to trust these officers to carry out their functions. That probably means in a voluntary association that they willingly draw work into their area of responsibility. They should get on with the job and not keep having to be chivvied by the chair and secretary. The chair needs to know that if Dolly has said she will do it, she will – by the agreed time and in the agreed way.

But there is conflict because at the same time the officers should not build empires or try and protect their area jealously. They should tell others what they are doing. They should be willing to let other people help. Sometime someone else will take over from them, so the way they do the job should be comprehensible to other people. You get someone who seems to cope absolutely reliably, then they move house or lose interest, and it is like unravelling a woolly to find out what they've done.

Another danger is that they forget what the association is for. They put everything into building up membership but in doing so get people who aren't really much use because they are not interested or are actually disruptive. A press officer thinks that all that matters is getting headlines, regardless of how the association is represented in the story underneath.

When someone takes over a post they should be briefed on what is expected of them. The same role is not expected of a publicity officer in all organisations: he could be in charge of relations with the press or responsible for getting out leaflets or posters, or simply expected to keep a watching brief for opportunities. Some deputy chairs simply deputise for the chair in meetings but he may take over one side of chair's general duties outside meetings.

A new officer should have his predecessor's papers and books handed over promptly. People lose interest once they are out of office and never quite get round to tidying things up to hand them over to their successors.

Responsibilities should be clear. The usual system of not being able to persuade anyone to take on a job and saying that Feisal and Cressida will do it between them, almost inevitably means that the job goes just like that – between them.

2.6 AN ORDINARY MEMBER

We are not all chairs, secretaries and other office-holders, not all of the time. Some of us have to be ordinary members, 'backbench' members of committees and meetings, the opposition, the people who come to listen, the people who come to argue their case from the floor of the meeting. How do we make our presence felt in committees and meetings?

I make some suggestions in this chapter from three points of view:

1. The people who are 'for' what is happening but who are either not powerful enough to have achieved office or are content to take a minor role;
2. Those who are 'against' what is happening;
3. Those who feel 'out of it'.

These are not fixed categories; we shift from one to the other according to the meeting and the issue.

I make some suggestions about involving ordinary members from the perspective of the ruling clique in Chapter 5.

FOR

You might think that nothing could be more straightforward than supporting an association's actions or its ruling group. There are problems:

– leaderships are remarkably unaware of their supporters, except when they get rattled and think they might lose a vote;
– supporters begin to wonder why they bother to come when everything is going OK.

Then, we don't turn up for a meeting or two and lose interest. Meanwhile, the people whom we support maybe lose a vote (because the opposition are more determined to attend) or fail to get a quorum and can't make decisions at meetings.

What advice? Mostly, I think, to recognise the problem, to realise that we need to be conscientious to prevent our side from crumbling away or being swamped by other factions. We can encourage ourselves to get more involved by:

– finding out more about the subject;
– joining in activities, even daft events like Halloween Balls;
– volunteering to work, like to take minutes, deliver leaflets, clear up;
– fawning on the leadership and drinking with them after the meeting.

When we do attend meetings, we can be dangerous by:

— babbling on and revealing the weakness in our side;
— being a thoroughly nasty person and discrediting our allies.

Sometimes under fire we should shut up and let our leaders speak. As the chair said to a new committee member,

> When I want your opinions, I'll give them to you.

It is a delicate balance between being on the winning side in a democratic structure and submitting to a tyrany.

Backbenchers and supporters come in several different forms.

The loyal sloggers
Some people are content to deliver leaflets, attend meetings regularly, work hard, be patted on the head by the leadership

> Great party worker, our Amelia. Sits there knitting, meeting after meeting, bless her; spoke once last year — bawled out that young Trot; always be relied upon to stuff envelopes.

Like gold-dust, they say, but usually ignored. When we are the foot-soldier or the Injun (among the too many Chiefs), we have to find our own praise. Go home and tell ourselves that but for us. . . . Face it, we have taken it upon ourselves. We have decided: that we can't all be leaders; that we should contribute some basic muck-shifting; that this is what we have the talent for; that we want to be needed somehow; that we want 'to belong'. Probably a mixture of the lot, with a feeling of martyrdom quite close to the surface.

I reckon anyone who holds a high-powered office ought to do some boring paperwork or knocking on doors, perhaps in another association.

Interested but not terribly involved
We recognise the association is a good thing, but find it difficult to sustain interest without being deeply involved and working. Are we really serious?

One word of encouragement if we would like to do more: don't wait to be asked — volunteer. Most meetings and committees consist of a few people wondering why the rest are apathetic and saying how they wish someone would show signs of being prepared to take more on. This is not entirely true (they are also keen to hang on to power) but we will get further by acting as though it is.

Sitters in
Many officers and powerful people in other organisations are content once a month to sit in as voting power or cannon fodder at another meeting. I listen to you at the Alternative Society; you listen to me at the Bypass Committee. Are we:

- the bane of committee rooms everywhere, deadwood committee professionals;
- part of a vital network of power?

Perhaps after months dormant we suddenly make the vital connection between one meeting and another, one project and another, carry a scheme through a council committee, distract a trouble-maker by drawing him into another group. But we should be checked every so often to make sure we are not stuck to the chair.

AGAINST

Some people oppose what is being proposed but basically are playing the same game. As in parliament ('The Loyal Opposition') or in local authorities ('the minority parties'), there may be sharp political division about what decisions should be made but a consensus about what issues are discussed and how. We disagree about selling council houses but we accept it is a real issue and match argument for argument head-on.

What are the tactics for opposition? I can only offer in this book a few, basically procedural points; this is not about how to present convincing rational arguments. What else can we do apart from speaking our mind and getting beaten in the vote?

When a motion is proposed, propose an amendment (see 3.6). It may be possible to swing over enough people to win an amendment which would in effect debilitate the motion even if we could never defeat the motion directly. At least, we can assess the strength of support for us – which will be useful information later – and we may confuse people and loosen up the other side.

Quibble with the wording of a motion. In a formal meeting use a point of order (see 3.11)

Order, Mr Chairman. . . . Is it in order to propose a motion which doesn't make sense. . . .?

If necessary and with a weak chair, cheat

Order, Comrade Chair. . . . Is it in order for the proposers to insult our brothers by their reference to. . . .

Or in a committee from under furrowed brows

I don't quite see what is meant by. . . .

Lay a false track, flap a red cloak. Any association has red herrings which will distract attention from the topic under discussion; in the confusion the meeting may grab any idea

It's not safe to go out at night. . . .
This women's lib is all very well. . . .
My three-year old daughter put it very cleverly. . . .
None of this would have happened under proportional representation. . . .

Play with procedural points (see Chapter 3). Moving 'next business' (see 3.7) can bring the house down. Know how to challenge the chair.

Play for time. Propose a 'reference back' (see 3.10) to the executive of a motion or to the subcommittee of a report

It's a worthy effort but raises problems. . . .

Set up a working party

. . . . complex technical issues. . . . important for the future. . . . not to be rushed into.

Probe – but indirectly – their insecurities, their failures to stand up for the interests which they represent, their previous commitments, their moral scruples, their aspirations to be seen as radicals or good guys, to be loved.

OUT OF IT

The straight opposition might be furious and argue desparately but they deal in the same terms as the people who run the show. More difficult is when we are alienated or disaffected. The meeting provokes – perhaps only afterwards – an incoherent bewilderment: That's not how it is.

Several things seem to happen:

– the debate rolls on quite logically to a decision which we don't like but we can't see where we could have actually stated our disagreement;
– the arguments are not presented in our terms, the language is not ours, the issues are not the ones most important to us;
– maybe, we even nodded agreement at the time but later realise that this is not what we think matters.

How can we join in? If we do speak up, it doesn't turn out right:

– we make a shrill emotional outburst (Stop the meeting, I want to get off); or
– we pitch it wrong. We mean to be moderate but it sounds like we're toadying to the bosses. We mean to be radical but everyone nods pleasantly and ignores us.

The debate may not even make sense to us. References to people, organisations and previous discussions fly around unexplained. Speakers seem to be talking in code. Fierce debate ranges over a minor technical calculation; mountains are made out of molehills, and vice versa. It's like visiting an old battleground where ghostly armies are still clanging and booming about. We daren't step into this: it might be a land-mine or a cow-pat.

Anyway no-one expects us to speak. We have no role established in these meetings. We are out of place. Perhaps we decide 'One speech won't change anything' and let the debate rage past us.

Or else, more normally, what we want to talk about doesn't get on the agenda. (The agenda is perhaps drawn up by a chair and secretary who are not open to suggestions.) Suppose, we know that the residents of Stucco Villas are building barricades against our organisation, but the only spot on the agenda to raise this is under 'Any other business'. By then half the members are packing up their papers and the others making a run for the pub before closing time. It takes real courage to hold back a meeting at that point.

What can we do?

Action in the meeting
Be aware what is happening. The way in which information is structured and presented does tend to fix the terms of the debate. Once people have heard a case presented one way, they find it harder to hear another point of view. This is a common phenomenon, not a product of our inadequate minds.

Speak firmly, early in the debate, preferably immediately after the main speaker(s), thereby making sure the terms of debate are set in our way.

Or, speak quietly, right at the end; appearing not to expect to influence the outcome but nevertheless to leave the impression of reasonable dissent with people. They may remember you another time and look to you to participate.

Or, speak disarmingly to defuse any hostility or resentment, unthreateningly

> I'm a newcomer. Can I just throw out for discussion some of my instant reactions to what's been said. . . .
> I've got to say that I'm a little bit worried about the way the debate has been going. Look at it my way. . . .

Consider how in committees you can plant an idea, nervously, casually

> What about a drawbridge?

Then step out of the discussion for a while to see if it flowers; some time later one of the powerful people says as though she thought of it herself

> A drawbridge would be lovely and very practical. . . .

Even if nothing happens, you have edged in and it's easier to pick the idea up later

What I was thinking about in suggesting a drawbridge. . . .

Shake the buggers rigid by speaking passionately for an oppressed group that they are unthinkingly trampling over. Though you probably will not win your point this meeting, they may remember you another time and look to you to participate.

Prepare for the discussion, even write out a complete speech, so as to feel secure at least in knowledge and command of issues. Few people really do give brilliant impromptu speeches; most have lain awake at night rehearsing them. Moreover, the people who are familiar with these meetings have had plenty of practice in speaking its language. We as outsiders have to prepare more carefully.

Prepare for the meeting by reading the agenda and the papers.

Know the rules which are used by the meeting. Play them at face value. Even if the regular members have got into the habit of shouting over each other to speak, we should raise our hands and try to catch the chair's eye. Probably the chair will remember the proper procedure; if not, we'll shame them.

Be brave; stop the meeting to get our bit in. Seize the chance of a relevant specific point to make a general statement like

This raises basic problems about. . . .

Be there. Groups tend to adapt to accommodate people and ideas that are actually present in flesh and bones.

A place
One way to get the confidence to speak up is to feel we belong to the organisation and have a role in it. Be prepared:

− to do chores, deliver leaflets, duplicate the newsletter;
− to volunteer for a position like minutes secretary that the ruling clique thinks a bore;
− to dig out some information that is needed for the next meeting;
− to sit on a working party.

It is possible to rise at amazing speed in voluntary associations, trade union branches and local political organisations just on the basis of volunteering to work. And perhaps by not making your own opinions too evident – if you don't say much, people think you agree with them. Hence, the opportunities for 'entryism' (according to which theory subversive Ultra-Left Marxists worm their way into the Labour Party by doing the chores that social democrats and democratic socialists cannot work up the enthusiasm to do).

Don't stay a lone voice, if possible. Build friendships and alliances, even if that means accepting someone else's view on trust occasionally. Identify with a group outside the meeting; you could be a loner in a committee but be recognised as spokesperson for a section of the community or an interest.

3 Procedure

3.1 PRINCIPLES

THE RULES

The purposes of meetings and committees are:

- to decide what to do;
- to come to a decision which is accepted as legitimate;
- more idealistically, to benefit from the ideas, skills, knowledge and opinions of the people present;
- even more idealistically, to do so in good time.

I discussed these purposes in Chapter 1.

In order to achieve their purposes, meetings and committees must be:

- properly constituted;
- properly conducted.

The rules are contained in the constitution of the association and in its standing orders or, otherwise, the conventions and common practice. In some associations the rules for constitution and conduct of meetings are all in one 'rule-book'.

Properly constituted
A constitution typically begins with 'objects clauses' such as

> The objects of the association shall be to provide hot soup for the distressed aristocracy of Fulham.

This statement is the basis for its existence and power legally; it enables it to act. The association is not allowed to act outside these objects (see 4.2).

The constitution says who can be members:

Membership is open to all living or working in Fulham and adjacent areas who are concerned for the welfare of aristocrats living in distressed circumstances.

It may add how members are to be elected and how they are divided into categories such as 'ordinary' and 'associate' members. It may also add, perhaps later, the provisions for disciplining and expelling members.

The constitution has thus provided the two pillars on which an association is built: the statement of purpose or objects; and, the statement of membership. An association is people joining together for a purpose, and the constitution and other rules are the statement of their agreement to do so and to run their business in agreed ways.

Alongside this, the constitution must also provide for changes to itself and for the dissolution of the association. Usually a change in the constitution requires a two-thirds majority (see 3.8) at a general meeting and may also require a straight majority vote in the executive committee. The way in which an association can be dissolved varies but will include provision for all members – and perhaps other people who benefit from the association – to participate in the decision. The constitution specifies how much notice must be given of these proposals.

The constitution describes the functions of the meetings and committees which run the association. It distributes powers and duties as has been considered most useful for the particular association. The annual general meeting of the association may be clearly given controlling powers:

The supreme governing body of the association shall be the annual general meeting, at which all members shall be entitled to be present and to vote. The annual general meeting shall determine the policies of the association.

Or, more typically for community associations, a rather lower key affair, the powers interwoven with those of an executive committee:

The annual general meeting shall receive the annual report of the executive committee and the annual audited statement of accounts. It shall make recommendations to the executive committee. It shall elect . . . members to the executive committee and appoint auditors.

Likewise, the functions of the major committee(s) are stated:

In furtherance of the objects of the association, the policy and management shall be directed by an executive committee.

The constitution says what officers shall – or may – be elected and by whom (see 3.9), and it may outline their functions (see 2.1).

The constitution sets out the requirements for holding meetings:

– the notice to be given of meetings (see 3.2);
– the quorum, the minimum number of people who must be present (see 3.5).

Properly conducted
The rules or standing orders describe how the meeting must be conducted. The main provisions are:

– procedure for debating motions and amendments, the heart of formal procedure though not now as all-pervasive especially in committees (see 3.6);
– procedures for electing officers (see 3.9);
– procedure for voting (see 3.8);
– mechanisms for controlling debates, such as 'points of order' (see 3.11).

Some standing orders go into great detail about the conditions for speaking (time-limits etc), for voting, for disciplining members and for dealing with all kinds of nightmares.

However, many associations, particularly pressure groups, do not bother to draw up detailed standing orders or rules. If the members are normally cooperative, it seems unnecessary to devise – and win agreement for – several pages of rigmarole. They, as I discussed in Chapter 1, can work on the conventions and common practice. The main points about the conduct of meetings and committees and for debating procedures are widely accepted.

The legal back-up

Do these rules have the force of law? Can we rely on the law to back us up in enforcing them?

As I discuss in Chapter 4, the law is rather ambiguous and ambivalent in this area. There are no laws which describe generally the procedure for meetings and committees, although companies and local authorities are specifically subject to laws which cover these matters. The law of the land can be applied to almost any situation somehow, however. You might invoke the law if, for example, you believed an association had taken action outside its constitutional powers (ultra vires – see 4.2) and had broken its own rules in coming to a decision. Then, in general terms the courts could be expected to uphold the decisions of properly constituted and conducted meetings and to allow an injunction against improper or illegal actions. The courts may, however, find it difficult to operate in the muddy waters of group politics if no financial concerns are at issue. They would also be likely to consider that broader principles of justice should take precedence over a strictly literal reading of the detailed rules of an association.

As well as the law many associations are subject to forms of public control which can be almost as binding. There are a number of commissions and public authorities which watch over the affairs of some associations, and to which associations submit either by joining or by nature of their status. Thus, for example, the Charity Commissioners watch over charities.

But the basic point is a political, even moral, issue that we have joined together in an association on the basis of its rules and that if we disregard them we are devaluing the association and breaking our agreement. It is a curiosity of the law that we cannot be certain that a court would care, as I discuss in Chapter 4.

BEHAVIOUR

The power of the chair

The chair

– is in charge of the meeting, but
– can be overruled by the meeting.

The chair's perspective on a meeting has already been discussed in

Chapter 2.2. Within the constitution and rules the chair has authority over the meeting, and much is a matter for the chair's discretion. The chair

— opens the meeting (unless the chair has to be elected);
— progresses the meeting through the agenda;
— selects speakers;
— conducts votes;
— rules on matters of order;
— ends or adjourns the meeting.

But there are limits. The meeting can

— challenge a ruling of the chair (see 3.11);
— approve a resolution calling for a speaker whom the chair has ignored to be heard;
— vote for a procedural motion (see 3.11) for example, that an item or motion should not be considered;
— and, in some cases, continue a meeting if the chair has adjourned it unreasonably (see 3.11).

The members

The conventions for members' behaviour are based on those of the House of Commons — though this assertion rings hollowly since its proceedings have been broadcast on the radio. A principal feature is that all remarks should be addressed to the chair (Mr Speaker in the House of Commons). Thus statements and questions are directed to the meeting rather than to individuals. It helps stop meetings from degenerating into personal chats or backbiting. It depersonalises the discussions (see Chapter 1).

It is also usual to insist on what the textbooks call 'parliamentary language' but what is really politeness, comradely discussion or restraint. People are not meant to swear at each other or simply swap insults. Thus, it is probably proper to ask 'May I through the chair ask whether the meeting considers the previous speaker to be a habitually reliable source of information . . . ?'. But it would be out of order to suggest 'Ted, you're a bleedin' liar and you always have been'.

The trouble with 'parliamentary language' is that these elaborate, indirect statements become a committee jargon. They make it more difficult for people who are not used to meetings and committees to join in.

Members are also expected to be well behaved. Only one person should speak at a time, and even a friendly committee should resist the temptation to break up into several private conversations. Members who wish to speak should indicate to the chair by raising their hand up or jumping to their feet as someone else stops speaking, and then they should wait until the chair selects them to speak. Some meetings insist that speakers stand up.

Confidentiality

How the ruling cliques have agonised! Can we trust them – the representatives of the clients, the parents, the students, the staff, the ordinary people, the community – not to go off and repeat every word we've said in committee? Us chaps realise that we're occasionally a little loose in our talk and know by instinct what it's appropriate to pass on. But do they have the decency/political skill/breeding or will they just blab it out? And then there's all this terribly sensitive material which we deal with . . . .

And so a great mystery has been made about confidentiality until people who are new to committees scarcely know if they are allowed to pass on any information about the discussions to the wider membership or their own group. In fact, much less is really confidential than is often thought. Some bodies do mark some items as confidential or even have a confidential half to the agenda. Some chairs make clear certain items are to be treated in confidence. Some committees have a tradition of being entirely confidential. In all these cases the members must respect the ruling – though they may argue for greater openness. Otherwise members need not feel constrained in reporting back and in passing on information.

However, so strong are cliquish ideas, new members might do well to tread a little carefully, testing out how much detail people in different bodies tend to pass on outside the meeting. In one body a representative may report back regularly with

. . . and then Councillor Zed argued that in an ideal world all rock and roll singers would be flogged in public.

Whereas another – more typical – is more diplomatic

Councillor Zed (*or* A speaker . . .) thought the band should not be allowed to play.

And you may feel some loyalty to even opponents on committees and not therefore gossip about the meeting as freely as would be fun.

But these are points of politics and of politeness, not a powerful mystery about confidentiality. We owe loyalty and accountability not only to a committee or meeting but also to our constituency or the public, and so we have counterbalancing reasons to report except where an item or discussion is marked or agreed as confidential.

We should, I think, try and limit what we decide is confidential: personal matters affecting individuals, especially if unfavourable or (given our culture) financial information is involved; a few discussions where public knowledge would wreck the scheme, depending on the particular association; some cases involving legal proceedings. But not where we retain information to preserve our power or to avoid embarrassment and having to explain ourselves.

Declaration of interest
Again, a mystery is often created about a technical detail.

We need to know as members of a committee if other people are, or might be thought to be, influenced in a discussion by an outside interest, especially a financial interest. So if Councillor Zed has shares in the company which supplies the equipment for public floggings, he should declare that interest before he advocates public floggings. Otherwise, we would have assumed his proposal was purely in the interests of the association or the welfare of society.

The convention is that Councillor Zed should say as the item is raised

Can I declare an interest, Mr. Chair.

He would then only take part in the discussion if asked or in a circumspect manner. He would not vote. Some rules are more specific and may even require the member to leave during the discussion.

Apologies for absence
Members who are unable to attend a meeting should write a brief note of apology to the secretary. The names of members who have apologised are read out at the beginning of the meeting.

MEETINGS AND COMMITTEES

I pointed out in Chapter 1 that, although for many practical purposes it is not obvious, there can be a difference between a *meeting* and *committee*. There are major distinctions in procedure. A meeting is more likely to be conducted strictly according to rules or standing orders which are formal and even ceremonial, whereas a committee operates in a more relaxed, less constrained style.

Distinctive features of a meeting are commonly:

— that the chair is, or claims to be, entirely non-partisan and does not participate in the discussion, making only procedural statements (see 2.2);
— no business is conducted except on the basis of a motion (see 3.6);
— a motion must be proposed *and* seconded (3.6);
— there is a strict order of debate with speeches for and against the motion (3.6);
— speakers stand.

Corresponding features of a committee are:

— that the chair may join in the discussion;
— business can be discussed as a topic (rather than speeches for and against a motion) and if an agreement is going to be formalised into a motion, then it can be worked out during the discussion (rather than presented at the beginning);
— motions only need to be proposed;
— speakers can remain sitting down.

In a meeting a member can only speak either as a speech on a motion or amendment (and can only speak once on a motion or amendment, subject to being called by the chair to speak), or can rise on a point of order or point of information (see 3.11). Whereas in a committee the members join in when they can (subject to the chair) and can contribute ideas and suggestions.

In practice in many associations, particularly pressure groups and community groups, the distinction may exist in terms of the difference between an annual general meeting and committee meetings, but is often blurred. Sometimes committees are rather more formal, and it is their subcommittees which have the more relaxed style.

The strict procedure of a meeting that business can only be done when a resolution has been proposed and seconded is cumbersome and uncomfortable but it does help concentrate the mind and produce a clear statement of what the meeting or committee intends. Committees very easily talk around a topic. They come to what they think is a consensus that, say, the rock band would be alright if the local tenants agreed – only to discover when the band is playing that the members of the committee were mostly opposed to it but had not actually thought it would ever happen. Committees are prone to leave issues hanging in the air, particularly when they have officers or workers to whom they can leave the decision. The old joke is that a camel is a horse designed by a committee, but it is more likely that the committee rather liked the idea of a big animal which could carry trees with its trunk but they left it to an executive officer to sort out the details.

3.2 CALLING A MEETING

Well, you ring round your friends and let them know.
Wrong!

The rest of the book is worthless unless the meeting is properly called. All the claims about democracy, collective action and fairness are nothing if the people who are entitled to be at a meeting do not know when and where it is happening and what it will discuss. A notice of a meeting must be sent to all who are entitled to attend.[1]

Many associations are slap-happy about this. The secretary forgets or the duplicator breaks down, or the stamps are too expensive, or Jo who promised to deliver the notices leaves them in the glove-pocket of the car. However, if a meeting is not properly called, its decisions could be challenged later and invalidated or – better – the meeting could not be allowed to begin.[2]

The method of calling a meeting is commonly described in a clause in the constitution. For a school governing body it is included in the instrument of government, and this indicates its importance: it is part of the main statement about the body rather than a detail of its procedure.

Usually the constitution requires that a number of days notice of the meeting is given. This is often 'five working days' or 'seven clear days'.[3] It probably also specifies how frequently the body must meet – once a year, once a term, at least six times a year etc. For example, the instrument of government of a local education authority's schools requires that meetings of governors are held 'not less than once in every term' and that they are summoned by sending an agenda 'so that it may, in the ordinary course of letter post, be delivered at the address of each governor at least twenty-four hours before the time of the meeting'.

A constitution also says how members can demand a meeting even if one is not scheduled or planned by the secretary, as

A special general meeting shall be convened at the request in writing to the secretary of ten members. Such a meeting shall be held within 30 days of the request.

It is normally the responsibility of the secretary to send out the notice of the meeting (see 2.3). It must be sent to everyone entitled to attend: for a general meeting of an association, to all its members; for a committee, to all members of the committee.

The notice must state clearly the date, time and place of the meeting. This is not as easy as it sounds. It was, for example, completely obvious to the organisers that 'The . . . Clinic' did not actually mean the venue was the clinic itself but rather the building where the clinic used to be, now given over to a free school and ethnic jewellery market, but I got lost. Never underrate people's capacity to be confused about times and places.

The notice must state the nature of the meeting and its business, and often the agenda (see 3.3) is made part of the notice, as

There will be a meeting of the Recipe Subcommittee of the Fulham Association of Soup for Aristocrats at 6.30 p.m. on

Tuesday, 13 November 1979 at 5 Dead End Close, London, SW6 to discuss the following business:
> 1 . . . . .
> 2 . . . . .
> 3 . . . . .

Associations may fix a string of meetings, perhaps a whole year in advance. It looks rather pompous when in January people get out their diaries

> Sorry I can only make Tuesday in the third week in October, or Thursday for the following week. And November is pretty busy.

It is also possible that as the year unrolls you find you need meetings fortnightly for a while and then only every two months. But otherwise it can be surprisingly helpful to choose a regular day each month or to fix several meetings in advance, especially if you are involving local councillors, union activists and committee hacks.

3.3 AGENDA

The agenda is the list of the topics to be raised at a meeting and the order in which they are to be discussed. It looks something like this:

1. Apologies for absence
2. Minutes of the last meeting
3. Matters arising from the minutes
4. Correspondence
5. Report from Finance Subcommittee
6. Report from Membership Secretary
7. The Ark – arrangements for sale of tickets
8. Petition from residents of Primrose Way
9. Motions (Full texts attached)
10. Any other business

The agenda is usually drawn up by the secretary, perhaps in consultation with the chair or other officers (see 2.3). It should be

sent out with, or as part of, the notice of the meeting by the
secretary, together preferably with any reports and subcommittee
minutes. The agenda

— determines what is discussed,
— gives shape and order to the meeting,
— acts as a timetable or progress-chaser for the organisation.

The form of the agenda depends on the way the particular
meeting operates, whether mostly through reports of officers and
subcommittees, through discussions of topics or through debates
on motions. A committee which is running a club or organising
activities on which there is general agreement may seldom
consider motions, except in the broad sense of approving what
has been done and authorising the next steps. By contrast, some
trade union meetings proceed through most of the business by
considering formally proposed motions.

Only the items which are on the agenda can correctly speaking
be discussed at a meeting, and the chair can rule out of order any
attempts to raise other issues. This is to prevent your neighbourhood fanatic turning up at the meeting, counting his mates and
pushing through his private fantasy. People are entitled to know
in advance what items will be discussed so that they can prepare
themselves and even make a special effort to come.

The decisions about which items to put on the agenda are
therefore crucial, politically and administratively. The early parts
of the agenda are, however, fairly automatic. If there is no chair,
the first item must be to elect the chair for the meeting. Likewise, it
may be necessary to elect a secretary to take minutes. The next
item may be a procedural point about the composition of the
committee, such as a welcome to new members or an appreciation
of resigning or deceased members. Then — and this is where many
agendas normally begin — the meeting gets underway with
'Apologies for absence', 'Minutes of the last meeting' (see 3.4) and
'Matters arising' (see below). (Some bodies do not write in
'Apologies for absence' as an agenda item: the chair is expected to
remember it; some bodies put 'Apologies for absence' after
'Minutes' and 'Matters arising'.) Next there may be an item
'Correspondence' or 'Communications' when the secretary reports on incoming mail, notices of rallies, appeals for donations etc
(see below).

The organisation of the rest of the agenda may take more thought. Most bodies continue with business items and the reports from officers or subcommittees ('Treasurer's report', 'Report from Finance Subcommittee' etc.) and put debates about topics and motions lower down the agenda. Debate about juicy issues can be unending, and most associations prefer to make sure there is time to get through the regular business first. The danger is that you talk all evening about, say, the Government's foreign policy or the local police, then realise as everybody is leaving that you have not approved the annual accounts or the purchase of new stationery and therefore the organisation is about to collapse or the chair can't write a dignified letter to the newspapers. Hence, agenda usually have 'Motions' or long debates near the end – it limits the time available for them. I suppose that generally this is sensible but it shouldn't be done automatically. It is just as easy to debate a choice of duplicating machines at length or to spend the first two hours of every meeting on the 'Treasurer's Report' and find that the real work of the association is skimmed over. This is deadly if you're hoping to maintain the interest of anyone other than the committee hacks. So, the agenda could (after 'Matters arising') go straight into the meat and hold back boring business to the end. The danger then is everyone leaves after the interesting bits (on account of baby sitters . . . victory celebrations in the pub . . . despair) and you lose your quorum (see 3.5) for approving expenditure.

Whichever of these structures you follow, there is skill in placing items in sequence. Do the people on this committee find it easier to go from general policy to detail or vice versa? Will it be more logical for them to discuss the Government's policies for their area of concern before or after the question of their redundancy payments? Do you as a ruling clique plan to use the voting on arrangements for the annual outing as a test of the support you are likely to get on the more important issue of next year's programme? Consider also whether any items will be confidential (see 3.1). If they are grouped at the end, people not entitled to be present can leave. Some agenda are divided into non-confidential and confidential parts.

The last items on an agenda are 'Any other business' and, if not already fixed, 'Date of next meeting'.

Agendas have some flexibility. An item left off, forgotten or urgent can be raised as 'Any other business', 'Correspondence' (i.e., by having a letter written on the topic and sent to the secretary), or as an amendment to a motion or emergency motion. However, a chair would probably not allow a large and controversial issue to be decided under 'Any other business' or 'Correspondence', and there are likely to be special provisions for emergency motions (see 3.6). It is also possible to challenge the chair's handling of the agenda (see 3.11).[4]

The chair can with the agreement of the meeting change the order of items on the agenda. Thus if it looks unlikely that there will be enough time to discuss an important item at the end of the agenda it can be moved forward. Likewise, if there is a visiting speaker or expert who the committee only needs for one item, it is selfish to keep them waiting throughout the meeting.

Although the agenda can be politically contentious, for most associations it is more crucial that items come onto the agenda in good time. As I discussed in Chapter 2.3 on the secretary's role, neglecting to take a decision in good time can seriously mess up a planned activity, a constitutional change or the Christmas bazaar. If an issue has to go to the local council meeting in November, does that mean it has to go through its Development Committee in October, your Executive in September and your subcommittee in July? The agenda should both look backwards to check that progress has been made and forwards to anticipate forthcoming decisions and events.

In drawing up agenda these judgments are made:

– the fairness of allowing even opponents to have their say – or the political wisdom to see worse would follow by shutting them out or the confidence to know you can beat them in a straight vote;
– the timetabling of decisions and the scheduling of reports which are due;
– the shaping of the agenda so that items appear in a logical order.

Styles
Agendas can take several forms. The largest difference is between the bare, most formal style

1. Minutes of the last meeting
2. Matters arising
3. Correspondence

4. Reports
5. Motions (Attached)
6. Any other business

and the more open style, typical of pressure groups

1. Apologies for absence
2. Minutes of the meeting on . . . .
3. Matters arising
4. Report by Publications Subcommittee
5. Organisation of public meeting on . . . .
6. Discussion of Secretary of State's letter about . . . .
7. Report back on meeting with Chief Executive of local authority
8. Motion: 'That this association affiliates to the National Society for . . .'. Proposed by . . . .
9. Any other business
10. Date and time of next meeting.

A step in pushing a meeting towards decisions is to add a line saying what it is being asked to do

To note for information
To receive report and approve recommendations
To debate motion proposed by. . . .

There are more detailed variations. If the organisation does not require meticulous formal statements, the agenda itself can include a paragraph or a sentence under each item outlining the issues. Another form of agenda leaves a right-hand margin in which to record decisions and actions. This always looked old-fashionedly clerical but has made a dynamic come-back as people have realised it is useful to pin down who does what.

How to keep track of discussions and decisions in a body which needs to refer back and forth to previous meetings? One device is to number items in sequence throughout the year: the agenda of this meeting might begin at item 139. Or meetings can be numbered: 16.5 means item 5 at meeting 16. In dealing with a mass of subcommittee minutes, one sequence of numbers can be imposed on the whole lot for each meeting: Buildings Subcommittee's minutes begin at item 56. An annual sequence and subcommittee sequence can be combined by adding a letter-code: BSC 34/13 is item 13 at the thirty fourth meeting of Building Subcommittee. Thus the proposal for the location of the dart-board could be numbered 16.5 or BSC 34/13 and referred to by that number throughout a sequence of meetings. The in-crowd never mention 'dart-board'; they just ask 'What about BSC 34/13?'

One way to streamline business for those meetings which work mostly through receiving and approving long reports or minutes of subcommittees is to approve on the nod as much as possible and to put aside until the end any items which members want to oppose. It looks a bit untidy and it does mean members have to remember why they objected $2\frac{1}{4}$ hours ago, but it may enable the committee to rush through a lot of straightforward business.

Matters arising
After approving the minutes there must be an opportunity to raise matters which arise from them. The members ask: 'Was the statement sent to the press – I didn't see any coverage?'; 'Are the lights now turned off at 10.30 p.m.?' The officers report: 'As you instructed, the guard-dog is now taken for a walk in the park each afternoon'; 'Lack of time has prevented us from . . .'. However, 'Matters arising' is a potential procedural disaster. It easily slips into a discussion of what the previous meeting discussed. People look through the minutes, see something that grabs them and launch into an argument. But 'Matters arising' is intended for reports on action and developments, not for debates, and should not deal with matters which have been put down as separate items later on the agenda. If a committee gets stuck in discussing 'Matters arising', the meeting is messy and people get disgruntled because after an hour and a half they are still on item 3 of the agenda. When the next meeting spends most of its time discussing 'Matters arising' from the 'Matters arising' at the last meeting, all is chaos. I suggest it is useful to call this item 'Matters arising from the minutes which are not raised later on the agenda'. If the meeting has some items which crop up regularly, list them as separate items on the agenda. Keep 'Matters arising' for progress-chasing on minor and occasional activities.

But meetings which are regularly progress-chasing on a small range of activities can use 'Matters arising' differently in conjunction with the idea of numbering meetings and items in sequence.

Then (as above) item 5 in meeting 16 appears under 'Matters arising' at meeting 17

16.5 Location of dart-board: No progress on consultations with the architect.

When meeting 23 still includes 16.5 under 'Matters arising' you get a clear idea of how long it is taking.

Correspondence
In a pure and simple system the secretary reads all letters and communications received since the last visit and the meeting decides on action: Letter from . . . (noted); notice of demonstration to protest against . . . (decision on whether or not to send delegates); request for contributions to the . . . appeal fund (collection taken at meeting); final reminder on electricity bill (passed to treasurer for action); leaflet about . . . fete (noted); and so on through maybe a dozen or more items. Some provoke fierce discussion; some are of no interest at all.

The advantages are that the secretary reports all letters, notices and other communications, and so members hear of suggestions, complaints, news from other associations, campaigns, keeping in touch with the full range of activities. Members may also write to the secretary and so have points raised under 'Correspondence'. The process can be useful for an association without a vast quantity of mail, and with officers who are not expected to work on their own initiative.

The disadvantages are that the discussion is usually unproductive and takes too much time. The issues are raised haphazardly and without warning, and people are told enough to provoke a reaction but not provided with the preparation and structure for a decision. The secretary has had a duplicated letter from the Little Wetknees branch of the Campaign for Truth and Justice and you have to make a snap judgment on whether and how you should support it. Then you trudge through a heap of fairly irrelevant notices, suddenly hearing slip by one of the causes which you think is most significant. If the secretary reads clearly and says what the correspondence is about, it takes an age. If he rushes through it, all you hear is a blurred chanting of letter-headings. Stop, did the secretary just mention the dates of the Flower Show, a charter on nuclear energy, a newsletter about a liberation movement in South America?

Better, I think, to decide which correspondence is worth an agenda item in its own right or which can be raised under a related discussion. And, if an item on 'correspondence' is essential to open up other points, the secretary should be trusted to select those which are most important.

3.4 MINUTES

The minutes are the record of the meeting. They are essential

- legally because if there was any dispute about what the association had decided you would refer back to the minutes of the relevant meeting as the agreed and authoritative record;
- practically because the association needs to remember what it decided from one meeting to the next, as a record of progress and as a way of not making the same – or slightly different – decisions every meeting or so.

Minutes are not like journalism where everyone knows that facts in a news-story are not the whole truth and can be argued about endlessly. Minutes, once they have been agreed (see below), are not just one person's story of what happened; constitutionally, they *are* what happened.

Minutes are often an improvement on what was actually said. In writing up the meeting, the secretary tidies up a discussion. A skilful secretary can turn a rambling discussion and a vague consensus into a series of clear main points and a purposeful decision – or into such a perverse piece of fiction that you are speechless at its nerve.

A record is vital if decisions are to have status and legality. Without the record in the minutes a person could be held politically or even in some cases financially liable for what they claimed they did on behalf of the association. It is frequently a legal requirement that minutes are kept and made available, if requested, to 'watchdog' bodies (see 4.1) and members.

When the general meeting asks the management committee 'Why are you spending all your time on the swimming gala?' Or the executive asks its representatives 'Why did you tell the regional meeting that we thought. . . .?' Or the committee questions the officers on the decision to buy a brand new washing machine when they could have had the second-hand one from the lady-down-the-road for £25. Then you refer to the minutes where it should say something like:

> It was agreed to buy a Galactic Starblinder Z97 and to decline Mrs. Burden's kind offer;

or

> RESOLVED: The chair of the management committee be authorised to take action necessary to improve laundry services speedily.

And if two months after the above resolution there is no new machine and no sign of the laundry improving, the members check back in the minutes and see that it was the chair's responsibility to act. They call the chair to explain.

So good minutes are an important feature of the operation, of making progress and checking that decisions have been put into effect. They are not just a way of adding to the stock of used paper in the world.

CONTENTS

The form of minutes varies enormously. Some are so brief and formal that they are incomprehensible to anyone who was not present and deeply involved in the business. Some are long records of everything said. Some are summaries in note-form of the main issues. Some are like short essays on each topic, which anyone could read for general information.

In principal, the form and style of minutes is likely to reflect the association and its work. However, similar bodies with similar tasks may use very different conventions. Compare the form of these edited extracts from two local authority education subcommittees and the quantities of information they carry:

ENROLMENTS 19 . . / . .
The Principal reported on the number of students enrolled at the College for the session 19 . . / . .
Resolved – That the report be accepted.

The Training of Teachers for Further Education.
We received details of the contents of the Department of Education and Science's Circular No. 11/77 which .... In particular we noted that the report recommended .... We also note that the Secretary of State regarded the proposals .... However, the Government had doubts .... It was also seen that .... We therefore decided that ....

What is essential?

The minutes must record all decisions taken. They must record all motions and amendments which were formally put to the meeting (even if they were withdrawn or defeated) (see 3.6). In many bodies the minutes must record the names of the proposer (and seconder) of a motion or amendment and also the numbers voting for and against or abstaining (and sometimes even the names).

Thus, depending on the way in which this body works, the minutes will say at minimum:

It was decided to send three delegates to national conference;

or

It was moved by Mr. Jones and seconded by Mr. Smith that 'This association send three delegates to national conference'. An amendment was moved by Mr. Brown and seconded by Mr. Nurdle 'That the word "three" be deleted and the word "thirty-eight" inserted.' The amendment was lost, 15 voting in favour and 25 against with 2 abstentions. After discussion, the motion was then carried by 30 to 5 with 7 abstentions.

The first example would be sufficient for committees of most pressure groups and community associations but a more formal statement may be customary or required in some bodies. Even in more relaxed organisations the exact record of the resolution and voting figures can be useful to stop people becoming too cosy and woolly.

For most bodies the minutes must also record those present and those who have sent in apologies for absence.

What is useful?

That depends on the particular body. It is useful to refer later to the reasons why a decision was taken. Hence, the main points could be summarised:

> The advantages of a Galactic Starblinder Z97 were stated as . . . . ;

or perhaps

> Proposing the resolution Mr. Jones said that, in the past, three delegates had been found to be a suitable number as it allowed one to keep an eye on events in the conference room, one to lobby in the bar and one to stay in bed to recuperate from a hard night's lobbying . . . . Proposing the amendment, Mr. Brown said that if democracy was to have any meaning in the association it was vitally important . . . .

Associations which use minutes as progress-chasers between meetings need an immediate and unambiguous note of who is going to do what. Thus:

> TOWN HALL DEMO Banners – Jo and Eve; leaflets – design approved, Cressida to get printed (within £ . . . limit); sandwiches – Wayne . . . .

Confidentiality

Some decisions are confidential to the committee or the organisation. If the agenda is split into confidential and non-confidential parts (see 3.3), the minutes follow the same format. If the association has a minute-book (see below), the confidential points may be recorded there but not in duplicated or printed versions of the minutes; the latter says 'See minute-book for full record'.

TAKING AND AGREEING MINUTES

Minutes are taken by the secretary or, if there is one, by the minutes secretary or by a 'volunteer' who happens to have brought a pen. Many meetings begin by bullying someone into taking minutes – it seems a chore.

The person taking the minutes jots down the decisions and usually the main points of the discussion. He makes certain that he – or the chair – has the wording of motions and amendments and names of proposers (and seconders). The minutes-taker may find it necessary to break in at the end of a discussion and say 'What do you want me to record?'. Because people who volunteer to take minutes are shy, conscientious types, this is sometimes difficult, but it often produces the most constructive part of a discussion.

Usually the minutes-taker writes up the minutes after the meeting, though if you are familiar with the association you can complete simple minutes as the meeting proceeds. If he is inexperienced or uncertain, he may consult with the chair or secretary about the format and wording, particularly where discussions are to be summarised or the political scene is confusing. Much is said off-hand in friendly meetings that doesn't fit the public face needed in the minutes.

The minutes are submitted by the secretary to the next meeting. They may be duplicated or printed and distributed, or they may be read out at the beginning of the meeting. The minutes of the previous meeting are usually the first or second item on the agenda (see 3.3).

The meeting has to agree that the minutes of the previous meeting are correct. This is not an opportunity to discuss whether what is written in the minutes is what you would like to have been decided at the last meeting; it is simply a question of accuracy. Mostly, corrections to the minutes are like 'Could I point out, Mr. Chair, that my name has an "E" on the end'. If corrections are acceptable to the secretary and the meeting, the chair writes them in and initials them. If there is disagreement, then an amendment to the minutes must be moved (and seconded), leading to a discussion and a vote. When corrections and amendments have been resolved, the chair asks 'Do you agree that I should sign these minutes as a correct record' or asks for someone to formally propose (and second) 'That the minutes be signed as a correct record'. If there is still disagreement, then the chair holds a vote. When this is resolved, the chair signs the minutes. The chair's signature authenticates the minutes constitutionally as evidence of what was decided.

Some organisations have an actual minute-book, maybe handwritten. Sometimes they do this for propriety and also send out duplicated copies; sometimes from economy, not wishing or being able to afford to send out copies. If—as is now usual—duplicated or photocopied copies are sent out, it is important to keep a master set, maybe bound into a file, signed by the chair.[5]

If it will be a few weeks before a meeting to approve the minutes, some bodies compile an action-sheet of decisions as a progress-chaser until the next meeting.

Variations

Normally, meetings and committees confirm – i.e., correct and agree – their own minutes, as described, but there are different practices.

There is a common tangle about approving subcommittee minutes. Subcommittees submit their minutes to main committees – often this is the form in which they report and have their decisions confirmed (see 3.10). Suppose: there is a meeting of Stationery Subcommittee on 15 February; it submits its minutes to the main committee on 26 February; but Stationery Subcommittee meets next on 12 March; can it then decide the minutes submitted to main committee (on which action might have been taken) were incorrect? This can be a touchy subject in bodies where subcommittees have a wider membership than the main committee.

At the opposite scale, what about minutes of annual general meetings and conferences? Do they have to wait until the following year to be approved?

Practices vary. Many associations do have subcommittees confirm their own minutes, and AGMs confirm theirs, despite the potential problems. An alternative is to have the main committee approve subcommittee minutes so that the subcommittee does not itself confirm its minutes. Likewise, the meeting of an executive committee may be empowered to approve minutes of general meetings and conferences. Another alternative for subcommittees and, more so, working parties is that at the end of a meeting they agree the minutes which will be passed to the main committee; the minutes secretary does his work on the spot.

WRITING MINUTES

The form and style of minutes vary from organisation to organisation, their customs and the preference of the minutes secretary.

The main difference is whether the minutes are confined to a plain statement of the formal decision which was taken or record the discussion which led up to it. If the latter, do you summarise the main issues anonymously or report what people say by name? And in how much detail? Reporting what people say by name has pitfalls: any report which reduces a speech to a few phrases is liable to distort; people get very sensitive. It is most difficult in committees where one person may make several contributions, but in formal meetings where people give set speeches it may be expected and easier.

How does this organisation operate? Does the chair lean back powerfully and announce 'Well, we seem to agree on the main points. We can sort out the detailed wording for the minutes afterwards'. Or does each item end by the chair summarising the discussion? Or does the meeting work through formally proposed motions? Some meetings sound as though they run for the benefit of the minutes secretary, frequently stopping to clarify what has been said – and no bad thing if it means that the members then realise what they have agreed. Does this organisation use its minutes for progress-chasing between minutes? Does it want them to be accessible to outsiders? Does it treat them as sacred text?

Some illustrations may help demonstrate different styles and the opportunities for the minutes-taker. I have used a scene from *Antony and Cleopatra* by William Shakespeare. It is not, as Shakespeare wrote it, truly a committee meeting but the form and development of the discussion is very like one. It is the meeting of the triumvirate which ruled Rome – Caesar, Antony and Lepidus – when Mark Antony returns from messing about in Egypt with Cleopatra. Caesar is gunning for Mark Antony but the discussion smooths out the differences, and the meeting decides that Mark Antony should marry Caesar's sister, Octavia.[6] Suppose it is a committee meeting, the minutes of the previous meeting and apologies for absence having been taken; item 3 on the agenda is the discussion of the split in the triumvirate . . . .

A fairly full set of minutes recording the issues might read:

3. *Triumvirate: cooperation*
There was a full discussion of past and future cooperation between the triumvirate, particularly concentrating on possible misunderstandings between Caesar and Mark Antony. Caesar raised three issues: 1. he feared Mark Antony had encouraged

the attack on Rome by Pompey and Fulvia, Mark Antony's wife; 2. he was concerned that Mark Antony had rejected his envoy in Egypt; 3. he wondered why Mark Antony had denied him military assistance despite the terms of their treaty. Mark Antony replied to these issues: 1. he had not been informed about, much less involved in, the war against Caesar; 2. when the envoy first called he had been temporarily indisposed and overtired following intense diplomatic activity, but nonetheless he had engaged in full and frank discussion the following day; 3. his denial of military assistance should be interpreted as an unfortunate oversight due to his preoccupation with affairs in Egypt. During the subsequent discussion it was widely thought that the current military situation confronting Rome demanded that past differences of opinion be put aside. Agrippa then proposed, 'That Caesar should offer his sister, Octavia, in marriage to Mark Antony'. It was argued that this would bind Caesar and Mark Antony in perpetual amity and an unslipping knot. The resolution was approved unanimously.

Compare a different style and a pro-Caesar slant:

3.   Mark Antony – suspicion of treason
In response to Caesar's charges that Mark Antony had conspired against him and refused to provide military assistance, Mark Antony apologised. He admitted his actions were the effects of a decadent life-style. He committed himself to supporting Caesar in future and agreed to marry Caesar's sister, Octavia, to prove his loyalty. RESOLVED: That Mark Antony should marry Octavia.

More diplomatically:

3.   Triumvirate – continuing solidarity
Caesar noted some current rumours about Mark Antony's situation in Egypt and the civil war in the Mediterranean. Mark Antony noted that he had been preoccupied with diplomatic activity on behalf of Rome in Egypt but that henceforward he would be entirely committed to the war-effort. Agrippa proposed that Mark Antony should marry Octavia, thereby reinforcing the constitutional and military relationship with more personal ties. The committee agreed to this proposal unanimously.

But some styles of minutes do not include notes of the discussion:

3.   Government of Rome (Triumvirate)
Resolution: 'That Caesar should give his sister Octavia in marriage to Mark Antony' was proposed by Agrippa. It was agreed unanimously.

Occasionally, minutes do not even include the wording of the resolution at this point on the grounds that the wording was given in the agenda for the meeting:

3.   Government of Rome (Triumvirate)
Resolution, proposed by Agrippa: AGREED.

All the above examples, even arguably the last, include the essential information about the decision. The following style is wrong:

Caesar and Mark talked about the latter's experience in Egypt. Enobarbus described in graphic detail how Cleopatra went on a barge.

Shakespearian scholars will immediately realise what's wrong, apart from the failure to record the decision and the lack of hard information. It is, of course, that Enobarbus' speech ('The barge she sat in like a burnished throne. . . .') is made after the meeting is over and should therefore not be included in the minutes, even though it is dramatically and politically a crucial statement. It's like 'No. No-one did actually say that at the meeting but we were talking about it in the pub afterwards and I thought it was important.' With a good minutes secretary, who needs Shakespeare?

3.5 QUORUM

A quorum is the minimum number who must be present for the meeting to conduct its business. It is stated in the constitution or rules (or the articles of association for a company or local government legislation). Typically the quorum of a committee is set at about a third of its members, while the quorum of a meeting, such as a union branch, may be about one-tenth and larger associations are likely to fix a smaller number. Some committees which are carefully constructed of representatives of different constituencies specify that the quorum must include a number of representatives of this or that body.

The meeting cannot start until it has a quorum. Normally everyone waits for, say, fifteen or thirty minutes for latecomers, but if there is still no quorum the meeting is adjourned. Under some rules, if the meeting has been called in response to demand by members, it would be abandoned or dissolved rather than adjourned to another day.

If people leave during a meeting and it loses its quorum, the chair should adjourn the meeting.[7] It is common, however, particularly in unions or community groups where there is some business to be done, for the meeting to be continued informally noting that there is no quorum and requiring that all decisions are ratified by the next meeting.

But often it is not up to the chair to notice that the quorum has been lost. Conventional practice in committees is that a member has to 'challenge the quorum', that is to draw the chair's attention to it. Until someone does so, the meeting can proceed in order (with the wise old hands hoping that some young enthusiast doesn't blurt out 'I don't think there's a quorum'). Once someone has challenged the quorum, the chair must check the number present. If indeed there is no quorum, he adjourns the meeting – or maybe continues informally as above. Some associations have rules which state 'no business shall be transacted unless a quorum be present' (or some such), in which case it is the responsibility of the chair (or perhaps the secretary or clerk) to ensure that a quorum is present.

Not to state the quorum breeds confusion and may open the way to unrepresentative minorities.[8] Ideally, a quorum is the point of balance between ensuring full representation and actually getting some work done.

3.6 MOTIONS AND AMENDMENTS

The heart of procedure is the rules or the practice for debating motions and amendments. It is this, with its basis in parliamentary procedure, which most clearly distinguishes the formal meeting or committee meeting from a simple business meeting or unstructured group. It is also the ability to handle this procedure which most clearly distinguishes the political in-crowd from the rest – whether the in-crowd learnt the groundrules in a school debating society, the Oxford Union, the National Union of Students or by regular attendance at union or party meetings. Yet to the newcomer it is a strange way of doing things, like watching a mystical cult in action.

PROCEDURE

In rigorous, formal procedure for meetings no business can be done unless a motion has been proposed (and seconded). Unless it has been, there is nothing to discuss. The end of the world may be scheduled for 11.45 p.m. but the meeting cannot discuss it until a motion – I would guess an 'emergency motion' (see below) – has been proposed and seconded. According to the style of the association, it may be worded

This house believes that the end of the world is nigh

or

That this association deplores the spirit of defeatism appertaining to the forthcoming 'end of the world' and instructs its executive committee to negotiate with the Archangel Gabriel on the following points:
(a) . . . , (b) . . . , (c) . . . , (d) . . . , (e) . . . .

Many meetings, particularly committees, are not conducted quite so formally. The chair allows a discussion on the topic before the wording of a motion is worked out to summarise the proposals. Only then does the meeting switch into the formal procedure for taking motions and amendments.

Even in a meeting which is trying to be unpretentious, to adopt the conventional procedure for motions and amendments helps sort out a decision. After so much discussion a meeting gets like a whirlpool; everyone is slightly at cross-purposes; no one view predominates. Then, a tidily-worded motion with possible amendments can break the subject down into stages which can be agreed or rejected one at a time.

Suppose, for example, a wrangle about the beer to be stocked. It could be sorted out with a motion

That the bar be stocked with Watneys Special bitter

and amendments

(1)   Delete 'Watneys Special bitter' and insert 'Ruddles County'.
(2)   Add at end 'and Theakston's Old Peculiar'.
(3)   Delete all after 'stocked' and insert 'at the discretion of the barman'.

I work through this example below, and even though motions and amendments can be several paragraphs or pages long the same rules apply.

THE BASIC STRUCTURE

Before a motion can be discussed, it must have a proposer and a seconder – though in committees generally a seconder is not necessary. First, the chair reads out the motion and asks whether it is proposed (and seconded) and gets back a shout or a wave. Having ascertained this, the chair calls on the proposer to speak.[9] If the proper is not present, the motion falls and the meeting proceeds to next business.

In classic debating procedure, after the proposing speech the chair calls on the opposer to speak against the motion, followed by the seconder for the motion and then the seconder against the motion. After these set speeches the debate is thrown open to the floor, and the chair calls alternately for speakers for and against the motion.

But in most meetings the opposition is not organised in this formal, parliamentary structure. Then, after the proposer and, if there is one, maybe the seconder,[10] the chair opens the debate to the meeting. It is common for the chair to take speakers for and against alternately but in some meetings people speak whenever they can 'catch the chair's eye'.[11]

Only one person can speak at a time, and each person can only speak once in formal debates (more often, probably in committees), except to raise points of order or information (see 3.11).

These may be a time-limit on speeches,[12] or the chair may have discretion (see 2.2).

Eventually, when there are no more people wishing to speak or the agreed time-limit has been reached or the chair decides there has been sufficient discussion, the chair asks the proposer to sum up.[13] An important rule about a summing-up speech is that it must only summarise what has been said and answer arguments which have been raised in the debate. It must not include new material or new information – the proposer is not allowed to keep back some vital information until the opposition have no chance to reply to it.

Then the chair moves on to the vote, reading out the motion again so that members know what they are voting on. He counts or has counted the votes for and against the motion and the number of people abstaining from voting (see 3.8) and announces the result.

Amendments

Thus, the basic procedure is very simple. Amendments make it more complex, but only because they add a further layer, not because something different happens. A debate on an amendment is a mini-debate inserted in the main debate. It is to go off sideways to sort out a detail and then to come back to the main line of the argument.

An amendment is always taken immediately after the speech proposing the motion. If there are several amendments, they are taken one at a time then. So, after the speech proposing that 'The bar be stocked with Watneys Special bitter', the chair reads out the first amendment

Delete 'Watneys Special bitter' and insert 'Ruddles County'.

He checks it is proposed (and seconded) and calls its proposer to speak. After that, the chair throws open the debate on the amendment and takes speeches (for and against) as long as time is available or required. Then, the chair takes a vote.[14]

If the amendment is carried, the motion now reads

That the bar be stocked with Ruddles County.

The chair takes the second amendment in exactly the same way. If it is carried the motion then reads

> That the bar be stocked with Ruddles County and Theakston's Old Peculiar.

The chair then takes the third amendment, which is, say, defeated.
    Now all the amendments have been taken, the debate begins on the main motion,[15] that is the motion as it has been amended to read

> That the bar be stocked with Ruddles County and Theakston's Old Peculiar.

The amended motion may not be much like the one originally proposed; it mày have almost opposite effects; or, it may be simply a little refined. Because it has been changed, the amended motion does not belong to the original proposer but to the person who proposed the last successful amendment. During the rest of the debate it is her motion, and it is she (not the original proposer) whom the chair calls to sum up before the final vote.

Some details about amendments
If the proposer of a motion is willing to accept an amendment, the chair usually, providing it is uncontroversial, lets it be added without debate. Thus, before starting to debate any amendments the original motion might have been amended

> That the bar be stocked with Watneys Special bitter and Theakston's Old Peculiar.

If one amendment would make nonsense or contradict another, the chair can rule that the later amendment falls if the earlier is passed. For example, if the chair took first our third amendment and it was passed

> That the bar be stocked at the discretion of the barman

the chair could rule that the amendments which named beers fell without debate.

Amendments are not allowed simply to negate the motion. The chair should rule out of order an amendment

> Insert 'not' after 'be'.

Most associations allow some flexibility in debating amendments. A chair who is good at managing a meeting will take amendments in a sensible order, assess the implications of amendments and whether later ones should fall, and suggest drafting amendments which make sense of the amended motion (though the chair must not refuse to have debated a properly-proposed amendment even if it is untidy or ridiculous). There's nothing quite as frustrating as hammering through several complicated amendments and discovering the substantive motion is gobbledeegook. An irritable and over-literal chair will then comment

> Well, that's the motion you've passed. If it means there's no beer at all, it's your silly fault for not thinking straight.

A reasonable chair, supported by the meeting, will recognise that the meeting did mean to get some beer and find – in seconds and in front of thirsty hordes – a tidy wording close to the spirit and letter of what has been passed.

Remitting to Executive
In conferences of political parties and unions motions can not only be won or lost but also 'remitted to the executive'. If the proposers agree, the motion can – without being voted on – be handed over to the executive committee to consider. This device serves to save face on (a) well-meaning but unpalatable motions and (b) motions which the meeting seems to support but which are riddled with sillinesses.

Taken in parts
A motion which contains several separate parts can be voted upon in parts if the chair and meeting wish. For example, a motion may propose several courses of action, and some members may support most but not all of them. Then, rather than have the complete motion defeated, the meeting can vote separately on the different actions. This device can be abused to win back ground lost in amendments or to confuse the meeting into voting your way.

Formal motion
In some meetings which do everything by motions, a 'formal motion' is one moved by the chair. The idea is that it should be non-controversial – like paying tribute to a fraternal delegate.

A 'formal motion' under some rules, however, is a 'procedural motion' (see 3.7).

Composite motion

In large conferences with motions submitted beforehand a steering committee may composite similar motions (with agreement of the proposers). Thus, one motion is debated, instead of, say, six or a dozen about the same subject.

Withdrawal

During debate the proposer may wish to withdraw his motion – perhaps he sees its flaws or fears it will be shamefully defeated. He can only do so if the seconder and meeting agree.

IS IT IN ORDER?

You can't discuss any motion. A motion has got to be within the objects of the association and within its rules, and the chair should refuse to allow debate on motions which do not fit. The rules, particularly those for formal meetings, may also require that motions are submitted in writing before the meeting but allow for 'emergency motions' to be submitted during the meeting.

Out of order

Associations can only do what their constitutions enable them to do; anything else is 'ultra vires' (see 4.2). Thus, say, the Fulham Association of Soup for Aristocrats is not legally able to take decisions or act on, say, either traffic in Fulham or on distressed aristocrats in Battersea, except in so far as these things affect the distressed aristocrats living in their area. A chair who is faced with a motion (or an amendment) on such a subject should rule it out of order, not allow discussion of it and move on to the next item on the agenda. The chair's ruling could be challenged by the meeting (see 3.11), but a member who subsequently thought that the meeting had exceeded its powers could legitimately complain to a superior body such as the association's annual general meeting or even seek a legal remedy such as an injunction against the decision being put into effect (see Chapter 4).

Notice of motions

The rules of an association may require that any motions to be debated are circulated to members with the agenda (see 3.3) or, at least, submitted before the meeting. This can sometimes even apply to amendments, although associations are usually less strict about this, particularly where amendments can be justified as 'drafting amendments' (that is, to improve the wording without changing the sense). So, the chair would rule out any motions submitted at the meeting without the proper notice unless they were 'emergency motions' (see below). Committee meetings may not always require notice of the wording of motions but the topic must be on the agenda.

Emergency motions
Events can move faster than agenda and formal processes. Therefore where notice of motions is required, as above, the rules must provide for some motions to be debated as 'emergency motions'. The rules describe what constitutes an emergency motion; usually that it relates to circumstances of which people could not have been aware at the time when motions had to be submitted. The chair rules whether the motion is an emergency motion.

3.7 PROCEDURAL MOTIONS

The next layer of complications in debating motions is that members have procedural devices to cut short or shelve the debate. There are two common 'procedural motions': 'That the question be put' and 'That the meeting proceed to the next business'. They can be moved during debates about motions and amendments and effectively they interrupt the proceedings. The chair, generally speaking, has to give them precedence over the debate.

In principle these procedural motions raise business-like thoughts: 'Have we discussed this enough?'; 'Perhaps it would be wiser not to make a decision at this stage' etc. In practical politics they are tactical weapons: you can cut short a debate when you're in front; or if, say, you think you will lose a vote on the main motion, you might yet be able to persuade – or confuse – people into not taking a decision, and that leaves you to fight another day.

I discuss motions to adjourn the meeting in Chapter 3.11.

CLOSURE: THAT THE QUESTION BE PUT

Mercifully we are not always compelled to listen to a debate until, and long after, it has dried up. Although there may be time-limits on speeches or on the whole debate and although the chair usually has discretion to draw the debate to a close, an ordinary member too can propose 'That the .question be put'. If this motion is carried, it ends the debate on the motion or amendment.

You can't really propose this motion simply because you feel bored, but it is possible to sense that a number of people are shuffling and twitching or have drifted off. Or it is possible that you and your allies have agreed that the debate should be cut short, maybe to hurry through the agenda to a subsequent item, maybe to prevent Reginald Knutts-Payne getting a say.

Basically the procedure is simply for you to catch the chair's eye and say

I move, Mr. Chair, that the question be put

or a similar convention in some associations. It seems preferable to do this only as a speaker stops speaking, but some rules allow you to interrupt a speaker, and where there are no specific standing orders and no time-limits on speeches you may be driven to interrupting a speaker. If you are doing it politely and waiting until a speaker stops, you need to be more forceful than simply to stand or raise your hand in an orderly way – you need to jump the queue by shouting that you want to move that the question be put.

It is common practice that only those who have not so far spoken in the debate can move this motion, so that having had your say you can't shut down the debate. But under some rules and in more relaxed meetings, anyone can do so.

The chair is not compelled to take this motion. He can decide that you are being merely destructive and that there has not yet been a fair and open debate. But generally the chair is expected to. (Some rules only allow 'the question be put' after a certain length of debate.)

There is no debate of this motion, neither from you to justify the closure, nor from those who oppose it. The chair hears you move the motion (and asks whether it is seconded, if motions require seconding). He tells the meeting that the motion 'That the question be put' has been proposed (and seconded) and then takes a vote.

If the motion is lost, the debate proceeds. If the motion is carried, the chair proceeds to close the debate, calling for the mover's summing-up on a main motion, and then takes the vote. The meeting then moves to the next motion or amendment.

NEXT BUSINESS

Another way of stopping the debate is to move

That the meeting proceeds to the next business.

But this has a more drastic effect. Whereas 'the question be put' leads, if it is carried, to a vote on the motion or amendment which is being debated, 'next business' means that the meeting jumps straight to the next item on the agenda without voting on the motion at all. It ends the debate and leaves the issue unresolved. If you move 'next business', you are proposing not only that the meeting stops talking about a question but also that it does not make a decision.

The procedure is as for 'the question be put' up to the point where your motion is carried, though some rules allow a limited debate on your proposal. The chair then moves straight to the next item. (If 'next business' is moved and carried while an amendment is being debated, it does not apply simply to the amendment but to the whole motion.)

PREVIOUS QUESTION

This is a rare and erudite point of procedure which is allowed in some rules. I think it is too extraordinary to be used where you are working on normal conventions and practice, and even the constitutional authorities say it is not applicable to committees. 'Previous question' is a more extreme form of 'next business' in that it shelves any decision on the question. The motion is

That the original motion be not now put.

It implies that the original motion is not worthy of consideration, and, therefore, it leads to a debate about whether the original motion is worth debating. The curious thing is that when the 'previous question' is voted on whether it is carried or defeated the effect is to end the debate on the original motion. If it is defeated, there is then an immediate vote on the original motion (as with 'the question be put'). If it is carried, there is no vote at all (as with 'next business'). A chair who is confronted by a motion for 'previous question' should consider whether the meeting is likely to be happy with this fix; there is less pressure on the chair to take the motion than there is with the other procedural motions; but once the chair has taken it, one way or the other, discussion on the original motion is finished. This has four hundred years of parliamentary precedent behind it.

3.8 VOTING

After a debate the meeting makes up its mind by voting. Usually the chair takes charge of the voting arrangements; in elections it may be the secretary (see 2.3). It is important that before people actually put their hands up (or mark their ballot slips) the chair makes it clear that they know what they are voting for. She should read out the motion or amendment (or the names in an election) at a speed they can follow. She may add some explanation, though this is dangerous if you are suspected of trying to influence the outcome. Likewise, the chair may need to clarify what is 'for' and what is 'against'. People not used to formal procedure are easily confused that in debating amendments a consistent line may mean sometimes voting 'for' and sometimes 'against'. In the example I used above, someone who was 'for' the original motion (Watneys Special) would have voted 'against' the amendment (Ruddles County), and then when Ruddles County won and became the main motion he would have had to decide in the final vote whether to vote 'for' Ruddles County or 'against' (and maybe risk no beer at all). The chair can clarify (if she can get away with it)

> Those who vote for the amendment will be supporting the trendy trotskyite real ale freaks.

The chair should take a vote clearly, slowly and neutrally.
Once the chair has announced the result of a vote, unless there

is an immediate demand for a recount (or whatever the particular standing orders say), it is final. Mistakes cannot be rectified. If you discover that you accidentally voted the wrong way, you cannot ask for the vote to be changed or taken again or for the result to be invalidated. Even if a chair was accidentally and in good faith to miscount the votes, the result cannot be altered later.

Quick definitions of two terms often used: 'unanimously' means that everyone votes one way, either for or against; 'nem con' means that some people have abstained but that all the others have voted for the motion.

METHODS

There are several ways of voting.

A clear agreement
The chair may realise that more or less everyone agrees. Then she can say

Is it agreed that the motion is carried/defeated?

She pauses for breath and unless there is protest or uproar she announces

The motion is carried/defeated.

Out loud
Some associations make a practice of having members shout out their vote. The chair says

All those in favour say Aye

and then

All those against say No.

She judges which side has most supporters. This is alright when the result is clear but if it is close the chair or a member can ask for a show of hands to count votes.

In defence of this method it is argued that people feel more involved in the meeting if they can shout out 'Aye' or 'No'. The great roll of sound of an overwhelming vote gives a sense of solidarity.

By hand

The commonest method is for members to raise their hands and be counted. In a small meeting the chair counts the votes for and against, followed by those abstaining from voting. In a larger meeting the chair appoints tellers to do the counting.[16] There may not be a need to actually count. The chair may see that the great majority are in favour or against and announces

The motion is overwhelmingly carried/defeated

or

The motion is won/lost by a large majority

or some such phrase.

If the chair does this, members have a right to ask for the votes to be counted; if there are standing orders or rules, they may prescribe how. It can be difficult for a chair in a large meeting to judge between two shows of hands. And it is not unknown for a chair to see roughly similar votes for and against and then announce very confidently that the side she prefers has won 'by a clear majority'. If she is going to do this, she should do it quickly so that the members do not have time to look round and see for themselves. Therefore be suspicious of a chair who hurries a vote.

When the votes have been counted, the chair announces the numbers for, against and abstaining. If they are close, a member can demand a recount; if there are standing orders or rules, they may prescribe how. When this second vote is taken – and possibly even a third or more – people are not really meant to change their minds and vote in different ways, though some will and nothing can be done about it. The last count is the decisive one: you can't decide that you preferred the first vote. In meetings of representatives or delegates, it is probably only those who have cards who are allowed to vote. They may be required to hold them up visibly when voting.

Card vote

A 'card vote', 'block vote' or 'poll' normally means one where representatives or delegates cast a vote not as themselves but on behalf of their so-many members. Thus a meeting which on a show of hands could split 105:98 in terms of those present could show an entirely different result on a card vote – maybe 389,000:505,000 – because among the minority of delegates were some who were backed by a larger membership.

A meeting which can have such an elaborate device as a card vote will have detailed standing orders or rules which govern the circumstances in which it can be held and the procedure. It may be possible to run a card vote by having tellers walk through the meeting noting the numbers of votes, but it is likely that members hand in cards which record their votes and that these cards are counted outside.

Secret ballot

In a secret ballot people mark their votes on a form or piece of paper which cannot be identified as theirs. Where this is expected, a meeting could have special slips or forms prepared. Otherwise, the secretary can tear up little squares of paper as needed. In any meeting where you can't see what everyone is doing with their hands, it is advisable to use distinctive paper.

Secret ballots are common for elections as a means of protecting personality, friendship, integrity and so on. In an ordinary committee meeting to vote on a motion a secret ballot looks rather cloak-and-dagger, though it has advantages as an ordinary procedure. A secret ballot makes it much easier to exercise independent judgement on an issue – even not wanting to upset your boss or flatmate can influence how you vote. But politics is not only about independent judgement, and an open vote can be a test of loyalty or solidarity and provide a measure of accountability.

Lobby

A few bodies – the House of Commons, most notably – count votes by having members walk through different lobbies to show whether they are for or against. This occasionally proves confusing even in the Mother of Parliaments.

Recording names

Some bodies on some occasions record who voted which way by name. A member may be able to ask for it in order to display to the outside world his virtue or others' deviousness. In some associations constituencies or branches which send delegates want a record of how their people voted. The standing orders will say when and how.

Members who think a decision is wholly wrong in principle (e.g., ultra vires or dishonest) may ask to have their opposition recorded by name in the minutes. It is likely that they could use this in defence against legal remedies for negligence or improper use of funds, as well as making a clear political statement.

SOME COMPLICATIONS

Coopted members

Members coopted on to committees (see 2.1) do not have the power to vote unless the rules say they do – although in practice committees may be friendly enough to let them. It seems unfair and hardly likely to make coopted members feel committed but the difficulty is that coopted members (e.g. on a subcommittee) may not have the legal and political responsibility which other members carry.

Proxy

By some rules someone who cannot attend to vote can arrange for another to cast his vote. This can only be done where the rules provide for it; it is not an unwritten convention.

Two-thirds majority

Rules normally say that some motions require a two-thirds majority to be carried: amendments to the constitution; suspending standing orders; and perhaps other matters which are fundamental to particular associations. The intention is to ensure that there is very clear support. It means that two-thirds of those voting must vote for the motion (eight out of twelve, 67 out of 100 etc.).

Ballots of membership

Some associations' rules require that motions on even more sensitive or fundamental topics require not just the support of the meeting but of a majority of all members: in some unions a decision to take industrial action; perhaps the dissolution of the association. If so, the rules will specify how a ballot is to be carried out.

THE CHAIR'S VOTE

Does the chair vote? When? How often? Where there are standing orders or rules the voting rights of the chair ought to be specified.

The customary practice of a *meeting* is usually considered different from that of a *committee*. In a formal meeting the chair does not vote unless there are equal votes for and against a motion in which case she casts her vote for or against and accordingly declares the motion carried or defeated. However, it is sometimes said that, if the chair is elected just for the meeting from among delegates, she retains her ordinary votes and has a casting vote as chair.

In committees of local authorities and companies the chair usually has two votes: one vote which she casts with everyone else in the ordinary vote and a second or casting vote if the votes for and against are equal. And many voluntary associations adopt this system of a 'casting vote', often expecting the chair not to have (in the rules) or use (by tradition) the first vote and therefore only having a casting vote. This is common, but the constitutional authorities are clear that the chair only has a casting vote if the rules say so; it is not accepted as an unwritten convention.

The practice is further complicated by habit of many chairs of not voting, even if they are entitled to, in order to demonstrate their impartiality. Some even refuse to use a casting vote, believing that if the motion does not attract sufficient support to gain a majority it should fail.[17] Many chairs use a casting vote not simply to follow their own preference but in support of the status quo or the leadership, just as traditionally the Speaker in the House of Commons votes for the Government if votes are tied.

In cases where the chair has two votes, they cannot be used together. The chair must cast his first vote with everyone else and only then if the votes are equal use the casting vote. And if he does not use his first vote, he cannot use it later. He cannot, say, cast two votes when the vote shows 20:19 in order to change the result to 20:21.

Casting votes cannot be used in ballots for elections.

3.9 ELECTIONS

Officers, committee members, delegates, deputations, all have to be elected. This is when long knives and short friendships become public property, when the future of associations are carved up and historic alliances chopped to pieces. What can stir the imagination like watching a 'slate' of candidates being well-managed in, say, a transferable vote system (see below) so that the voters' preferences are shifted from one candidate to another? What can compare with sorting through the results after the event to see how the CP backed a Conservative to scupper the SWP? How ever could more than 100 cardinals come to an overwhelming majority for a rank outsider as pope in only half a dozen ballots – and do so twice in a couple of months? That is real politics.

It is not always so. In many groups nobody wants to bother to be secretary, or else the whole committee is too wrapped up in other committees to have time to even type up the minutes. Elections turn into volunteering, cajoling, bullying, even being held over to the next meeting so that someone can find a candidate. That, too, is real politics: the look of she who wouldn't mind being pushed to volunteer; the disappointment of he who is ignored; the reasons why they accept; the satisfaction of being acknowledged by friends and allies. That, too, is real politics.

Against the political and emotional turmoil are set the rules and conventions, which provide the structure for fair play or public justice. There are several different forms of elections.

NOMINATIONS

Basically there are two ways of running an election: at the meeting or by post; sometimes nominations are collected by post for voting at the meeting.

To have a candidate stand for election normally requires:

– a proposer, and often a seconder;
– a seconder;
– the consent of the person (not to be forgotten);

—and maybe conforming to criteria about membership of the association, representativeness of the constituency etc., as laid down in the rules.

In the meeting
The chair or secretary calls for nominations for the post(s). As names are shouted out, she records the names with their proposers, checking if necessary that they are seconded and recording the seconder's name. She should check that the candidate is willing to stand or, if he is not present, that the proposer is certain he is willing. When the supply of names has dried up, she asks if the list can be closed or else takes a motion 'That nominations close'. The chair or secretary then reads out the list.

It is quite common in small, friendly organisations for people to keep an eye on the number of posts to be filled and for the number of nominations to match it exactly. Then the chair can announce

We have six nominations for the posts of six committee members. May I declare them all elected.

There follows a roar of approval or disconsolate muttering that there was nobody else willing to stand, and thus the six are formally elected.

On the other hand if there are insufficient candidates for the number of posts, then those who are nominated are elected. The remaining places are left vacant.[18]

If there are more candidates than post(s), then there has to be some form of vote. First, the chair or secretary must read out again slowly the list of names or preferably writes them on a board, so that everyone knows who is standing.[19] This is absolutely vital where members have more than one vote each.

Before the vote takes place, some associations have hustings in which each candidate speaks or answers questions for a short time. Sometimes the proposer says a few words about his nominee. This is embarrassing but useful; there are few associations where the members know everyone well.

One election is taken at a time. So that the result of the election for chair is known before the election of vice-chair, etc. When a number of people, say, committee members or delegates are required, then one election is held for them all.

When a meeting elects a committee (or a committee elects a subcommittee) there are two systems:

– to elect the officers plus a number of committee members;
– to elect committee members and leave it to the committee to elect its own officers.

This sounds like nit-picking but presents spectacular constitutional problems (see 2.1).

By post

Some associations ask for nominations for the election of officers and committee members to be delivered some time before the meeting so that the list can be circulated, printed on ballot papers or simply known to the organisers. They may hold the whole election by post.

Large delegate or representative meetings usually require this and have detailed rules. This seems sensible for smaller and less formal associations, too, particularly where many members do not come to the general meeting to elect the committee, but it frequently is a source of difficulty. The main difficulty is that, although people might be willing to stand, they and the association are so unpushy that no-one actually does anything about it, so that the association arrives at the general meeting without nominations as required by the rules. It is faced with the quandary of bending the rules and taking nominations on the spot or having a separate election later entirely by post.

The arguments about postal ballots or ballots in meetings are a running controversy in trade unions. It is commonly argued that postal ballots favour the 'moderates', not to mention the ignorant, the disinterested and the uncommitted. It also means that the membership relies on the written election address or second-hand reports from their activists. On the other hand, can someone elected by a small meeting claim the confidence of a larger membership?

VOTING

There are two basic procedures – by show of hands or on ballot papers. The latter are essential for some forms, like transferable votes.

Voting is always done *for* rather than *against*. Even if you are electing six out of seven candidates, it is probably against the rules and certainly unpleasant to cast votes against one person. Usually, if there are, say, six posts, each voter has six votes. Incidentally, it is normally OK to vote for yourself.

There are a number of ways of voting. They attempt to cope with two problems:

– how to express the wish of the majority;
– how to do so within the time available.

The first is not a simple question of who gets most votes. Suppose Reg (Hard Line Moderate) gets 19 votes, Nigel (Trendy Lefty) 10 and Cressida (Good Cause Liberation Front) 14. Reg has most votes, but is it certain that the majority prefer Reg? If Nigel had stood down, would Cressida have picked up his votes too? With more candidates competing for a number of posts, it is even more problematic.

Simple majority (First past the post)
Whoever gets most votes wins. If more than one post is to be filled, then the top so-many candidates win. In the above example, Reg wins.

This is how MPs are elected. It is the simplest and quickest but, as in the example, not necessarily a good measure of the electorate's views.

Clear majority
To be elected the candidate needs a majority support from the meeting, that is more than half the votes cast. If no candidate has a clear majority on first ballot, the bottom candidate is taken off the list and another ballot held. In the above example, Nigel is dropped and there is a straight vote between Reg and Cressida.

With more candidates more than one can be dropped off the bottom where their combined votes are less than the next up the list. Suppose on the first ballot: Reg – 19; Cressida – 14; Nigel – 10; Linda (Nature's Way) – 5; Jeff (Faith in Fascism) – 2. Linda and Jeff are eliminated. The second ballot goes: Reg – 21; Cressida – 14; Nigel – 15. Cressida is eliminated. The final ballot results: Reg – 21; Nigel – 29. (If Reg on the second ballot had picked up all Jeff and Linda's votes, achieving 26 votes, more than half the total, he would have been declared elected.)

Exhaustive vote
A more tiring version of the above for electing several posts at once – three delegates, five committee members etc. Voting is done in rounds. Each voter has one less vote than the number of candidates in that round. After each round the bottom candidate is dropped until the required number remain.

Single transferable vote (STV)
Each voter can mark a first and second choice on a ballot paper. The first preferences are added up for each candidate. If any have a clear majority (as above), they are declared elected. If not, the bottom candidate is dropped and the second preferences on his voting slips redistributed.

   If the election is for more than one post, the second preferences of people who voted for successful candidates are added to the votes of the other candidates. As candidates have a clear majority, they are elected.

   This system means that everyone's preferences are taken into account. It has to be done on paper and is slower than counting 'simple majority' votes.

Multiple transferable vote
You get as many preferences marked in order as posts. Thus if six posts, you mark the candidate 1 through to 6. The first preferences are counted, someone elected or dropped, their second preferences distributed, etc., their third . . . .

Proportional representation
This is applicable where there are established groups or political parties. You vote for a party more than a person, and the posts are shared out in proportion to votes cast.

3.10 SUBCOMMITTEES AND REPORTS

Much of a meeting's business can be done through receiving and acting upon reports from subcommittees and officers. For complex organisations this is how their wheels are kept turning, though the procedure can seem like track upon track of confusion.

The main body receives from subsidiary bodies:

– information about how they have carried out instructions or
  delegated functions;
– information which will help the main body reach a decision;
– recommendations for action.
For example:
– the executive committee reports on its year's activities to the
  annual general meeting;
– the action committee reports to the executive on its proposals
  for running a campaign;
– a special committee or working party produces its recommendations to the management committee on how expenditure can
  be cut;
– the schools subcommittee presents its minutes to the education
  committee, including both information on how it has acted
  within the powers delegated to the subcommittee and recommendations on how the education committee should act within
  the powers reserved to the main committee;
– the bar subcommittee informs the management committee
  about the takings and recommends a bulk purchase of
  Bulgarian red wine.
Or in the case of officers and workers:
– the membership secretary reports to the executive on how many
  people have joined;
– the delegates report on the national conference;
– the headteacher reports to the governors on pupil numbers,
  truancy and curriculum developments.

The reason is that the main body does not have the time to
undertake all the business, particularly the detailed discussions.
Nor does it have the expertise. A subcommittee or working party
can comprise those members who are most involved in the subject
and may include also other experts and representatives of outside
bodies. Committees and meetings cannot do everything; some
tasks have to be performed by officers and staff instructed by and
reporting back to committees.

RECEIVING REPORTS

In some bodies meetings consist almost entirely of receiving reports from subcommittees and officers. A spectacular example was how the Senate of the University of London dealt with 863 items of business on 161 foolscap pages in 15 minutes – clearly it discussed few of these items.[20] More mundanely, an agenda can include

Report of Finance and General Purposes Subcommittee
Report of Bar Subcommittee
Report of Positive Experiences Subcommittee
Report of Working Party on the Constitution.

These reports can come to the main committee either as the minutes of meetings, as a written paper or as a verbal statement. A special committee or working party would probably produce a written paper, whereas a standing committee might simply submit its minutes. A paper from a special committee might include a 'minority report' from a member who dissented from all or part of it.

The Bar Subcommittee presents its minutes, which the committee flicks through, discussing some items (typically the relative merits of Gamsa and Kabernet among Bulgarian wines). Then the Chair of Bar Subcommittee moves 'That the report of Bar Subcommittee be received and approved', and there is a vote, if necessary.

Or the Bar Subcommittee through its chair or secretary has prepared a written paper of information and recommendations. This is likely to be an easier read than a set of minutes and to set out more comprehensibly the information about the failings and the arguments for the purchase of the Bulgarian wine. After discussion, the chair of the subcommittee moves the confirmation of the report, leading, if necessary, to a vote. If it is long or complex, it may be taken a paragraph at a time.

Often, it is less formal. The person responsible for the bar presents a verbal report, and after discussion the chair wraps it up 'OK, Bruce. That's fine. Stick at it and let us know next time how you get on with the brewery'.

The main body to which the minutes or report goes can:

– receive its report;
– refer the report back (or, remit it);
– accept or not its recommendations.

To receive a report is to confirm that it is an adequate statement overall. To refer a report back is to say 'Think again'; a polite rejection, in effect. It means that the main body thinks that the subject has not been dealt with satisfactorily.

Practice varies on whether the main body can amend a report (as distinct from its recommendations). One version is that the report can only be received (or not) or referred back – on the grounds that the subsidiary committee has detailed knowledge or rights over its own material. Another version treats each paragraph of the report as a resolution to be approved (or not) or amended.

After receiving the report, the main body can accept (or adopt) and reject its recommendations. They then become resolutions of the main body. Normally the main body can amend the recommendations.

For example, when a schools subcommitee presented its report to an education committee the minutes read:

REPORT OF THE SCHOOLS SUBCOMMITTEE

The Chairman of the Schools Subcommittee presented a report of a meeting held on . . . .

It was MOVED and SECONDED:–

That the recommendation contained in Resolution No. 39 "Publication of External Examination Results" be not adopted and that approval be given to the publication of external examination results in accordance with the suggestions of the . . . Association of Secondary School Headteachers'.

On being put the motion was carried and it was:–

Resolved–That the recommendation of the report of the Schools Subcommittee be received and adopted subject to the following:–

That the recommendation contained in Resolution No. 39 'Publication of External Examination Results' be not adopted and that approval be given to the publication of external examination results in accordance with the suggestion of the . . . Association of Secondary School Headteachers.

Note how the clerk in order to correctly give the wording of all motions decided to repeat the identical words within a few lines because there were two separate resolutions passed.

In this case, the chair of the school subcommittee has presented the minutes of his subcommittee and, probably, there was discussion of several items. Then, a member has spotted the resolution by the subcommittee on publishing exam results and spoken, perhaps as: 'Mr. Chairman, may I raise my misgivings about the proposal from the subcommittee. . . .' One can imagine then a discussion, leading to a member formulating the motion above (or, it might have been formulated before the meeting when the subcommittee minutes were distributed with the agenda for the education committee). The motion was proposed, seconded and debated and passed on a majority vote. Then, perhaps after discussion of other items on which there was no disagreement, the resolution to receive and adopt the report of the subcommittee subject to the altered proposal was approved, perhaps after a vote.

INFORMATION AND RECOMMENDATIONS

The recommendations in a report can be handled in several ways. The problem is often to distinguish what in the report is for information and what is a recommendation for action.

The chair's dilemma when subcommittee reports are presented is to prevent the main body rerunning the subcommittee's discussion, particularly where no recommendation for action is being presented. It seems right that a member of the main body should be able to ask a question and be answered by the chair of the subcommittee, but it is easy to slide from that into a free-for-all. With a volatile situation it is even easier. Suppose that since the Bar Subcommittee met a new cheap Moroccan wine has arrived, posing questions of politics as well as of taste and economics. This is mentioned, and everyone begins arguing, and the members of the Bar Subcommittee all join in (though they can discuss it at their own meeting in a few days' time) . . . . Let a committee get into this habit, and quite soon every meeting will be a rerun of the previous one.

To sort out this kind of confusion you need to be clear:

— what authority was given or what powers are delegated to the subcommittee or officer (see 2.1);
— what is it presenting as *information* and what as a *recommendation* for a decision.

Where the subcommittee or officer is reporting what they have done within instructions or delegated powers, they are simply informing the main committee. The main committee cannot make a different decision and really there is not much reason for it to discuss at all – though there should be enough openness to allow a bit of clarification or even the hope that it would be done differently another time. I make some suggestions on delegation in Chapter 5.2.

The responsibility for distinguishing between information and recommendations rests largely with the persón presenting the report (often the chair of a subcommittee). There are devices to help:

1. To present conventional minutes but to underline or mark recommendations which need approval;
2. To divide the minutes into two sections, one headed 'For information' or 'Delegated matters not for confirmation' and the other headed 'For decision' or 'For confirmation', or some such;
3. To present conventional minutes but to list at the end the motions which need to be approved, for example:

CHAIRMAN TO MOVE

1. That the report of the Development and Buildings Subcommittee be received and entered on the Minutes.
2. That in respect of the petition referred to in Item 1 of the report now submitted, the petitioners concerned to be informed . . . .
3. That approval be given to the appropriations from Education purposes to Housing purposes. . . .
4. That approval be given to the acceptance of the tenders for the works set out in Item 3 of the report now submitted . . . .

4. To establish at once which items in a report will be disputed by other members and to separate them to the end of the agenda. Then all uncontroversial business can be passed 'on the nod'.
5. In drawing up the agenda, to spot any recommendations in a subcommittee's minutes which relate to items on the main agenda and to feed them in there. Then the subcommittee's minutes/report are approved with the exception of those recommendations, which are debated with the topic on the agenda.

See also Chapters 2.3 and 3.3 on drawing up agenda.

Loyalty

Occasionally, members of a subcommittee have a crisis of conscience when its recommendation is put to the main committee. Are they committed to voting for the recommendations? Perhaps they have had a cosy meeting of a specialist subcommittee and shown what good chaps they are in understanding, say, the staff's problems, but then when they arrive in the main committee they meet political reality eye-ball to eye-ball and change their minds. This may be mean and cowardly but I don't think it is unconstitutional.

3.11 ADDITIONAL CONTROLS

POINT OF ORDER

A point of order is an objection made by a member about the *conduct* or *procedure* of the meeting. If a member thinks that the standing orders or rules of the association (or, if none, the conventions of debate) are being broken, he can raise a point of order. He is asking the chair to make a ruling that what is happening is against the rules and must stop. For example, a speaker may

— deviate from the subject;
— use 'unparliamentary language';
— break a rule of the association.

Or, the chair may, for example

—miss an item on the agenda;
—run an election incorrectly.

The member should stand (or put his hand up) *at once* and say as loudly as necessary 'Point of order, Madame Chair'. The chair must halt the proceedings, stop the speaker and ask the member to say what the point of order is. The member must do this very briefly—usually a sentence or two, perhaps referring to the standing orders—in the form of a question to the chair. The chair hears him and then rules

> Yes, the speaker must refrain from using obscene language about comrades

or

> No, the speaker has not violated Standing Order No. 58.

And then she calls the speaker back.

If the chair rules against the point of order, it is normal to accept the chair's authority, but if you are outraged—or if the speaker believes he has been unjustly treated—it is possible to challenge the chair's ruling (see below).

Points of order are intended so that members can ensure meetings are conducted properly. They are not about the content of what is being said. Even if the speaker is misleading the meeting, you would be wrong to raise a point of order about it. Likewise, points of order are not meant to be an excuse for a speech, and the chair should insist that the point is stated very concisely.[21]

In the tactics of debate points of order are sometimes used—wholly improperly—as a form of sniping, harrying and breaking the speaker's train of thought. Even in this way:

> Unscruplous member: Is it in order, Madame Chair, for the speaker to talk rubbish?
> Chair: Entirely in order. Sit down. The speaker can continue.

The chair is in a dilemma. She is meant to hear any point of order but sometimes she sees that 'points of order' are being raised merely destructively – as above – or frivolously. The chair has not really then got procedural weapons (other than the ultimate powers, see 3.12) but may express her annoyance or rhetorically ask the meeting whether it is happy with this silly behaviour. When the chair is talking, it is tempting to ignore them.

Points of order are particularly confusing during votes. Usually they are not allowed while the vote is actually being taken, but before the vote whilst the chair is explaining the arrangements this may be the last chance of a beleaguered minority to get a word in. It can create havoc unless the chair is steady.

POINT OF INFORMATION

A point of information is to provide a brief piece of supplementary or clarifying information to what the speaker is saying. Like a point of order, it is not meant to allow a speech or an argument. It must be relevant and brief.

It is common to take information during speeches but at the discretion of, first, the chair, and, secondly, the speaker. A member stands (or raises his hand) and says 'Point of information, Mr. Chair'.

Chair to Speaker: Do you wish to take information?

and then either

Speaker: No.
Chair to Speaker: Carry on then.

or

Speaker: Yes, OK. /It would be my pleasure, Mr. Chair.
Chair to Member: Can we have the information.
Member: Is it not a fact, Mr. Chair, that . . . .
Chair: Thank you. The speaker can proceed.
Speaker: As I was saying . . . . /I am grateful to my colleague. . . .

A point of information may be genuinely helpful or subversive:

Is it not a fact, Mr. Chairman, that whereas the speaker claims that Bull's Blood is the best Bulgarian red wine it is actually a Hungarian wine.

A point of information may be used by a previous speaker to correct the present speaker's misrepresentation of his case.

Under some rules, however, points of information are only taken between speeches. As a speaker sits down, the member tries to catch the chair's eye before he calls the next speaker. Consistent with this procedure is that if a previous speaker believes he is being misrepresented by the present speaker, he can raise a *point of explanation* during the speech. He rises to ask the chair's permission to correct the misrepresentation. Again, he should be brief and to the point; it is not meant to be a chance to say what you wish you had said or start a new argument.

CHALLENGING THE CHAIR

I have emphasised the authority of the chair. He is responsible for conducting the meeting. He rules on procedure. But parallel to this power is the power of the meeting. The meeting can overrule the chair and can even unseat or express its lack of confidence in the chair. These actions are not to be taken lightly for the ability of a meeting or committee to work depends to a large extent on the chair. But that is no reason for the meeting to tolerate unreasonable, undemocratic or incorrect action. (Mere stupidity is usually allowed.) The procedures are designed to protect the chair from casual or insubstantial challenges.

The first step in challenging the chair is usually for a member to stand and speak up: 'I wish to challenge your ruling, Mr. Chair' or 'I wish to challenge your conduct of the meeting, Mr. Chair'.

The procedure for the second step varies. Some standing orders specify that there must be a certain number of people – perhaps, four – who are prepared to support the challenge or that it is necessary to have a simple majority of the meeting vote to hear the challenge. In other associations the challenge needs only a seconder. So the chair ascertains whether there is the required support to hear the challenge. If there is not, the challenge falls, and the chair continues as before.

The third step is for the chair to hand over the chair to the vice-chair, secretary or other officer or senior member. Then, the challenger supports his challenge with a speech. The chair (now not actually in the chair) replies, justifying his ruling. Conventionally, there are no further speeches, and the acting chair proceeds to take a vote on the motion to uphold the chair's ruling. The fourth step is a vote, and the acting chair announces the result.

The chair, then, returns to the chair and puts into effect the decision of the meeting whether it decided to uphold his ruling or to reject it.

A chair may think that to lose a challenge is the end of the world – those once-loyal friends befuddled by young upstarts, those years of licking envelopes late into the night rendered as naught, the revolution at the door. It need be no such thing. Even a chair should admit to the possibility of error or misjudgement and should – I say piously – welcome the expression of democratic judgement.

It is possible for a chair – a self-confident one – to make a ruling in order to have it challenged and test the opinion of the meeting. An incident might arise on which the rules were unclear. A ruling followed by a challenge might be a convenient device to resolve the procedure, perhaps setting a precedent.

Things could be worse. It may not just be one ruling on which the meeting wishes to challenge the chair but his whole conduct of the meeting and perhaps of the association. Then there should be some procedure to move a motion that the meeting or association has no confidence in the chair or that the chair should leave the chair. Under some rules this may not be possible except by submitting a motion to the next meeting, or it may be possible as an emergency motion. It may be possible to interrupt the main debate to debate this motion. The chair should hand over the chair to another officer, and there is then a full debate according to the normal practice (see 3.6). The chair should have the right to put his case. There is a vote, and because of the seriousness of this motion it may require a two-thirds majority to be accepted. It is a moot point whether officers are compelled to resign if they lose a vote of no confidence. If the chair resigns or leaves the chair, the deputy or vice-chair takes over. If there is none, then an election must be held.

SUSPENDING STANDING ORDERS

I have sat in a meeting, heard a member propose the suspension of standing orders, seen it passed and assumed that we had now entered a wilderness where there were no rules at all. This is incorrect. The suspension of standing order refers to one or more specific standing orders which are proving an insuperable barrier to the progress of the meeting, though this is seldom made clear.

Suppose there is a standing order that meetings must end by 10.30 pm, but on this occasion important business will take a little longer. Or a standing order limits speakers to five minutes, but the subject is complex. Or a topic has arisen urgently which cannot be fitted into the procedures described for motions. Then, a motion to suspend standing orders can be moved and seconded from the floor, preferably naming the particular standing orders. The chair can refuse to take it if he is not convinced it is necessary. If he accepts it, the chair clarifies for everyone what is happening and puts it to the vote. It requires a two-thirds majority to be approved. Then for the length of the particular business – perhaps specified in the motion – the meeting can act more flexibly than the standing orders allow.

We should treat the suspension of standing orders as a rare emergency measure, however tempting it is. As I have argued elsewhere, the rules are the basis upon which we have joined in an association; undercut the rules and we undercut the association.

ADJOURNING THE MEETING

The commonest version of an adjournment is straightforward. If there is no more time but still some of the agenda to complete, the chair and the meeting agree for adjourn to another day. The reconvened meeting will continue to work through the same agenda.

Similarly straightforward is a decision by the chair with the agreement of the meeting to adjourn for a short while so that people can get a drink, go to the lavatory or watch *Crossroads*. Or perhaps cool off from an argument, or take time out of the meeting for some lobbying to resolve a tangle.

The chair also has discretion to adjourn a meeting because of disorder, again either to another day or for a short period. How this discretion is exercised is problematic. The situation might be clear in, for example, a meeting being deliberately disrupted by outsiders where the chair has the confidence of the great majority of members. The converse situation might be almost as clear if, for example, the chair threw a sulk because he was not winning and stalked off the platform, taking his few supporters with him: then the meeting would be entitled to elect another chair and continue. But suppose the disruption was not violent and that the disrupters were a significant minority who perhaps disagreed with the chair and leadership on policy or interpretation: can the chair throw up his hands, announce 'It's pointless to continue. I am adjourning the meeting' and leave the chair? Has he properly adjourned the meeting or simply walked out and left the meeting to elect another chair in his place? The meeting ought, in justice, to be able to resolve by a majority to continue and elect a chair for the rest of the proceedings, but it is arguable. The solution would have to be worked out, I think, in the context of a particular body. What do its rules say? To whom is it accountable? Who can mobilise what power? And if the whole edifice of its procedure comes tumbling down, does anybody care?

It is not only the chair who can adjourn a meeting. A member can move a resolution

That the meeting be adjourned

or occasionally in the form

That the chair do leave the chair.

She may specify the date and time for the reconvened meeting. The procedure is as that for moving a procedural motion (see 3.7). If it is seconded, it takes precedence over other motions. It is not usually debated, and the chair goes straight to a vote. The procedure can be used simply because the chair is too stupid to realise that half the meeting is asleep or desperate to watch the football. It can also be a tactical device to stop an issue being discussed when you are not ready.

3.12 DISORDER

THE CHAIR'S AUTHORITY

I have said quite enough about the power of the chair to run the meeting in Chapters 2.2 and 3.1. But what happens when a meeting, or some or one of its members refuse to accept the chair's order? When the constitution is about to be knocked down like a house of cards?

It is useful to remember that everything we are talking about is a convention or an agreement among people, and not god-given, a law of nature or a metaphysic of human behaviour. It is only how we have agreed or consented to do things. If someone refuses to accept its basis or goes berserk, the chair is armed only with a gavel (perhaps), a wadge of paper and whatever power and authority he can dredge up out of his own personality and reputation.

But, fashionable though this perspective is, such a desperate position is in practice rare. The person who is chair does not rely on his individual ability alone: his status, the sanction of his colleagues or comrades, as well as tradition and everybody else's expectations support him. The problems of dealing with disorder in a meeting are deeply set in convention; the laws of the jungle are a long way off. Even allegedly mindless trouble-makers are very often bouncing off the rules, and seeing how far they stretch.

The meeting relies on its chair to exert its authority. What actions are available to the chair within the conventions when faced with disorder? He must have previously established an expectation of proper constitutional action and trust in his chairing.

1. He points out that this isn't the way to do things – low key.
2. He says more firmly that this cannot be done and that the proper procedure is . . . .
3. More heavily, he calls the person to order: 'Order' or 'I'm calling you to order'. Though it may sound absurd, it is likely to work.
4. He appeals to the judgement of the meeting 'Is this the way you want to proceed?' or some such.
5. He calls the person to order again, maybe appealing to his better judgement.

These stages involve a progressively firmer assertion of the status of chair and of the authority vested in the chair by the meeting. The chair must be:

– obviously fair;
– clearly decisive;
– big enough to take it;

—able to treat it as a conflict between chair and disorderly conduct rather than between you and him.

If none of this works, read on.

THE RULES

Beyond these conventions there are no conventions about disciplinary actions which the chair can apply. Some associations have rules which allow the chair to impose penalties or report an offender to a disciplinary committee. Some associations have a procedure by which the chair can 'name' someone who is creating a disturbance, thereby suspending them from the meeting and perhaps reporting them to the body which they represent. An executive committee would probably have the ultimate sanction of excluding someone from membership of the association.

ADJOURNING THE MEETING

The chair is empowered to adjourn a meeting on his own initiative if he thinks it is too disorderly to continue. He may adjourn for a short, fixed time, perhaps to allow tempers to cool or a disturbance to be dealt with, or he may adjourn to another day (see 3.11).

The chair's dilemma is that people who are creating a disturbance might be doing so to stop the meeting reaching a decision. Adjourning the meeting can show that the chair will not stand any nonsense but it could be just what the dissenters want.

THE LAW

There are three aspects of law which can be used to defend an organised meeting: the organiser's right to ask someone to leave, deriving from law about trespassing; possible actions at a public meeting against someone who 'acts in a disorderly manner for the purpose of preventing the transaction of the business for which the meeting was called'; the police's powers to prevent a breach of the peace.

Trespass
The organisers of a meeting have the right, as the occupiers of the

premises, to decide who may and may not be present (whether they own or have hired the premises). Even though the public have been invited, the chair, on behalf of the organisers, can withdraw the invitation and ask someone to leave.[22] If the person does not leave when asked, they are trespassing.

Dealing with trespassers is not usually done by going to law: trespass is not normally a criminal offence, and suing a trespasser for damages is seldom appropriate. But the fact that the person is trespassing means that the chair has the right, if they refuse to leave, to have him removed from the meeting. And to do so using 'reasonable force'.

The chair should direct stewards to remove the person. It would be unwise for the chair to jump down and join in such physical activity. The chair is more powerful preserving some dignity.

The fact of a person's trespass would also be grounds for an injunction against his coming to other meetings.

Preventing the transaction of business
The Public Meeting Act 1908 established:

> 'Any person who at a lawful public meeting acts in a *disorderly* manner for *the purposes of preventing the transaction of the business* for which the meeting was called together shall be guilty of an offence' (my italics).

Most people have probably been to meetings where someone could be thought to be doing just this, but this section of the act is not to be applied against ordinary heckling, filibustering and creating confusion. The words have to be weighed up very seriously against the nature and extent of disorder.

Action under this provision could be that:

- the police prosecute, though probably only in extreme circumstances;
- the organisers and the chair prosecute.

More likely the provisions of the Public Order Act 1936 would be applied. If he suspects someone of committing this offence, a policeman 'may if requested so to do by the Chairman of the meeting require that person to declare to him his name and address'. If the person refuses or if the policeman 'reasonably suspects' that it is a false name and address, the policeman can arrest him.

So, a chair who was confronted by someone who refused to leave a meeting and appeared to be breaking this act could ask the police to take the person's name and address. If the person refused, the police could arrest him and charge him.

Breach of the peace
According to the Public Order Act 1936,

> 'Any person who in any public place or in any public meeting uses threatening, abusive, or insulting words or behaviour with intent to provoke a breach of the peace or whereby a breach of the peace is likely to be occasioned, shall be guilty of an offence.'

This is a substantially different matter. The initiative is not with the chair or the organisers but with the police, though the organisers could call the police. The police are bound to take action against an actual breach of the peace and have powers to arrest someone reasonably suspected of committing the offence. The police may also enter private premises if they have reasonable grounds for believing a breach of the peace is likely to be committed.

Procedure is now in the hands of the police. The police may be cooperating with the chair and the organisers, but it is not inconceivable that it is they whom the police are arresting.

NOTES

1.   In some circumstances a notice on a noticeboard (where people expected to find it) or in the press would be acceptable.

2.   The chair could adjourn the meeting, just as he would if there was no quorum. However, the rules of some associations state that the accidental omission of a notice to someone would not invalidate the meeting. Likewise, if a notice was – genuinely – lost in the post, the meeting would nonetheless be considered properly constituted. Under Company Law in some circumstances members can excuse the inadequacy of notice.

3.   You may think that Saturdays and Sundays should not count.

4.   At some conferences the agenda has to be confirmed. A conference

steering committee may announce its recommendations for the order of business and put this proposal forward for confirmation.

5. Minutes are so important as a record that if they are kept loose-leaf it is sometimes suggested the pages be numbered or the chair initial every page.

6. The middle section of Act II Scene 2 lines 17–158 in the New Penguin Shakespeare when the triumvirate are all on stage.

7. A few minutes may be allowed, as in the House of Commons, for people to be dragged back from the corridors and bars.

8. Constitutional authorities say that for a meeting without a fixed or finite membership more than one member present would enable the meeting to proceed, though Company Law requires three at a general meeting of a public company. A case in 1877 Re Sanitary Carbon Co established that, except in special circumstances, one person could not constitute a meeting. For committees, however, some opinions are that *all* members must be present and some that a majority, if no quorum is specified.

9. In a meeting of delegates or representatives of associations it may be an association or branch rather than a person which is the proposer, and one of its delegates or representatives speaks.

10. The seconder may 'formally second' at this point and reserve the right to speak later.

11. In large, organised meetings like union conferences names of speakers may be submitted to the chair before the debate begins.

12. Large conferences sometimes have a set of coloured lights to warn speakers: orange – your time is nearly up; red – stop.

13. Also known as 'right of reply'.

14. Conventionally there are no summing-up speeches with debates on amendments.

15. Also called the 'main question' and the 'substantive motion'.

16. Some rules require that tellers be supporters of different sides; some have them appointed before the meeting gets underway. Tellers can vote, unless the rules say not.

17. A few associations allow a motion to be 'not carried' if votes are equal rather than 'lost' or 'defeated'. In such rules 'not carried' allows the motion to be reconsidered at a subsequent meeting, whereas defeated motions could not be debated again for some time.

18. The election for the remaining places is held at the next meeting if that is appropriate. The rules may allow the executive to coopt people to fill places, and even if they do not say so, this is commonly done in small voluntary associations, pressure groups etc.

19. Watch for secret codes like the chair or secretary putting a full stop after the names of those they want their supporters to vote for.

20. Evidence submitted to the Murray Committee on the governance of the University of London, quoted in *Higher Education Review* Summer 1971.

21. If speakers have time-limits, time spent on points of order do not count against their allocation.

22. There may be a possibility that if the person had paid to enter he could sue for breach of contract.

4 The law and other public controls

4.1 GETTING IT RIGHT

The law we tend to think of as a stack of ultimate certainties. Long after meetings are over we sit around reassuring each other that 'if it went to court, the judge would say . . .'. Even if we admit our ignorance, we reckon that if we rang a lawyer he could spell out the answers for us.

Not so. The law in most of the area covered by this book is peculiarly uncertain. Even in a case concerning apparently basic points, you could not be sure of the outcome.

Historically the law has not been strong in this area. There is little legislation in terms of acts of parliament which directly affects it, other than the specific Companies Acts and Local Government Acts. You cannot turn up an act of parliament on, say, holding annual general meetings for community organisations. Thus, mostly we are affected by the build-up of case-law, that is the precedents and principles established in previous cases. Here the law's major concerns have been:

- the balance of rights and freedoms between the individual and the state (and statutory and administrative institutions);
- the protection of property.

Our major concerns, however, are:
- group action and collective responsibility;
- the protection of socially-based 'rights'.

The law has tended not to see things in the way that we do. Speaking very crudely, the courts might only have resolved a question of whether a body had a right to make a decision in terms of the implications for financial responsibility. Moreover, as I discuss in 4.2, the law seeks to pin this responsibility on

138

individuals (rather than groups), and many of the associations which figure largely in our lives do not even have an existence in law.

A further aspect of the uncertainty is that the application of the law here is changing. The body of law affecting public administration and trade unions has developed in the past 20 or 30 years, and some of it has more general implications. Acts of parliament and the courts have had to provide for the intervention of central and local government and the role of trade unions in our lives. Curiously, a consequence of the increasing quantity of legislation was during the 1970s a high-wire act by Lord Denning and other judges to maintain (their view of) the equilibrium between state and individual rights and freedoms. Thus, in some cases where the intention of the act seemed to favour central government or a trade union, the judges supported, respectively, the local authority or the individual (see Denning 1979).

There could be further developments in that the importance of voluntary associations in our lives will have increasingly, I reckon, to be coped with by the law. This could mean some redefinitions of collective and individual responsibilities. Such changes would not be based on absolute legal certainties but set in a continuing revision of ideas about society, freedom, the individual, the group and the collective.

Another way in which 'the law' in this area is not as we popularly imagine is that it does not on the whole go looking for trouble. There is no sheriff who rides out in a white hat with a six-shooter to clean up the local parent–teacher association. Obviously, breaches of the Local Government Acts, Companies Acts etc. are – to some extent – sought out by the police and the 'watchdogs' (see below) and prosecuted, as are fraud, deception and other criminal acts. But the machinery of the law is not bothered about, say, the proceedings of the executive committee of the Fulham Association of Soup for Aristocrats – unless it is kicked into action by somebody's appeal to the courts. Feisal believes that the chair was wrong in allowing a motion to be debated and passed which was, he thinks, ultra vires (see below), so he goes to a judge to apply for an injunction to restrain the proposed action (see below). But, Feisal might have decided to deal with the problem through a political manoeuvre or by demanding a general meeting to debate a motion of no confidence; no-one might have wanted to seek a remedy in the courts.

So the uncertainties about the law are fundamental. I must therefore emphasise the caution with which this section of the book should be treated. I attempt to provide some – temporary – signposts through a minefield. Beware: I accept no responsibility; the circumstances of a particular case are all-important.

Given all that, however, it remains most likely that if you run a meeting properly and fairly the courts will back up your decisions. Similarly, a court is likely to require you to abide by a constitution. In one of cricket's great sagas, in 1978, people who supported Geoffrey Boycott for the captaincy of Yorkshire won a High Court order that the chairman of the county club should hold a special general meeting to consider the motions which they had submitted.[1]

But what if . . . a vote is deliberately miscounted . . . an ultra vires resolution is passed . . . insufficient notice is given of the meeting . . . the chair refuses to take a motion which is in order . . . an election is improperly run . . . or, choose your own nightmare . . . ? What can you do about it?

One possibility is that the action is actually criminal – the accounts defrauded, etc. – and that therefore you report the matter to the police and leave justice to take its course, providing there is sufficient evidence.

Otherwise, the main remedies open to you are:

– to sue for damages;
– to go to court for an injunction, declaration or order.

You would sue for damages if there was an actual financial or material loss – maybe exclusion from an association on which you depended for your livelihood or an unfair distribution of funds.

But, most of the upsets which we fear, particularly in voluntary associations, are not criminal and do not involve material loss. They are intangible matters which might not create a fuss in the big wide world but which might be central to vital political concerns or to evening-after-evening of fierce debate in meetings. So, the chair did cheat in declaring a motion out of order – does the law care? Only just.

You could go to court for an injunction which orders that an action must not be carried out (or, less commonly, must be carried out). Members might seek an injunction to prevent an association's executive acting against a resolution passed at the AGM or entering into unauthorised expenditure. The usual course of action is to go to a judge in chambers for a temporary – 'interlocutory' – injunction until a proper court hearing can be arranged. The court's ruling is binding; to disobey it is to be guilty of contempt of court.

Other remedies might be available, though the law is not at all forthright in this area. A declaratory judgement could be made by a court to state the legal relationship between parties; it sorts out the rights of a case and provides a basis on which the parties can proceed, but it is not enforced by the courts. The High Court could issue an order of 'mandamus' which instructs a body or person to perform a public duty which they have refused to do, though only at the discretion of the court and if the court can see that there was no more appropriate remedy. More specialist remedies are applicable for local authorities and other governmental and public bodies: 'certiorari' and 'prohibition', by which courts can compel bodies to exercise legal duties or quash their decisions.[2]

The difficulties of dealing in this area are compounded by the problems of deciding whom the parties in a case can be. You may need to show that you have a legitimate interest in the case or that your common law rights are threatened. You also need to correctly identify in the eyes of the court who the defendants should be, who you are attempting to hold responsible, and this could be particularly problematic in an 'unincorporated association' (see below).

The courts will come to a decision on the basis of the law, the facts of the case and the constitution and rules of the association. The constitution and rules amount to an agreement or contract between the members: they regulate the relationship between the members, in effect the operation of the association. Members can expect it to be upheld in law. However, (a) the rights and wrongs of a case may not be as startingly obvious to a judge as they are to you, and (b) there are higher principles of law which may take priority over your particular rules:

1. The courts do not simply base their decision on the association's constitution and rules. Although they are the legal basis of the association, they are not treated as though they were legislation and subjected to detailed analysis of the text. It has been established that: 'Trade union rule books are not drafted by

parliamentary draftsmen. Courts of law must resist the temptation to construe them as if they were'.[3] Courts are likely to allow discretion, particularly where rules are vague, in the direction of reasonableness, flexibility, stability and order. In 1978, for example, the national council of the National Graphical Association declared an election for a national officer void and held a new ballot after it discovered a clerical error in counting the votes. The candidate who would have been elected on the first ballot if it had been compiled accurately asked the High Court for a declaration that he had been elected. It was argued that the rules did not specifically give the national council power to declare an election invalid or order a fresh election, but the judge found that the national council had this discretion.[4]

The judges' remarks in the Court of Appeal (25 January 1978) on the dispute in the Newham North East Labour Party when the Labour Party's National Executive Committee suspended its committees and officers are illuminating. Lord Denning examined the rules of the party and the relationship between national and local organisations but in refusing an injunction against the NEC's action also took into consideration whether to grant an injunction would help remove chaos or provide stability.[5]

2.   The courts will insist on 'natural justice' rather than the rules of the association if there is a conflict. The two tenets of natural justice are:

– that a person judging a case must not be biased or be a party in the dispute, summarised as 'no-one be a judge in his own case', in Latin 'nemo iudex in causa sua';
– that a person affected has the right to know any case against him and to put his case, summarised as 'hear the other side', in Latin 'audi alteram partem'.

Thus, even if your rules allow you to expel a member without a hearing, a court is unlikely to support you if that member seeks an injunction against his expulsion.

3.   The courts are likely to support actions done fairly and in good faith even if not strictly speaking specified in the rules. Company law, for example, places weight on the authority of the chair in conducting the meeting and declaring the results of votes on motions.[6] Likewise, courts have supported the rights of

meetings within the rules of their associations to conduct themselves and decide for themselves by voting how they wish to proceed.[7]

4. The law is still really happier dealing with financial and material matters than political rights. In the nineteenth century it was held that: 'Save for the due disposal and administration of property, there is no authority in the courts . . . to take cognisance of the rules of a voluntary society entered into merely for the regulation of its own affairs'.[8] In cases relating to trade unions the law, especially in the person of Lord Denning, has learnt to consider rules of voluntary associations and to protect the rights of contract in issues of expulsion, though the cases have been founded largely on questions of the 'right to work' as against expulsion from a trade union. Injunctions have been also granted to individuals excluded from an office where no financial interest was involved and in cases concerning union elections. Nonetheless, the judgements in this area have tended to be somewhat off-hand about political rights where no financial loss was involved.

5. The law can be an expensive and cumbersome way of remedying a situation. A voluntary association faced, say, with a former treasurer who won't hand over the books might apply for a court order, but is it worth the lawyers' fees, the personal stress, the time waiting for the case to be resolved? It could, if it suspected a fiddle, report him to the police, but will the association's petty cash grab the arm of the law? The judges and the police would really prefer us to sort our own problems within our own constitutional arrangements. Note the comment of Lord Justice Geoffrey Lane on the case of the Newham North East Labour Party, as reported in *The Times*:

> The courts existed as a last resort for members of a party or organisation who felt that the only way that they could assert their rights inter se was to ask the court to define what those rights were. They did not exist to give the kiss of life to a faction which was otherwise not viable.[9]

And of Mr. Justice Pain in an earlier case in the same epic:

> One of the factions in the dispute seeks to use the method of frequent applications to the Court as a means to assist it in

achieving its ends . . . It may well be that the long-term effect of litigation will be to destroy the organisation for which they profess concern.[10]

PUBLIC WATCHDOGS

Usually on a committee it is not actually 'the law' in the shape of the police or a court with which we come into contact. We deal with one of the 'watchdog' bodies which are entrusted with the administration of the law. Bloodhound, bulldog or corgi, they try to keep us on the winding and overgrown path of legality.

These bodies, registries and commissions have generally been appointed by the relevant Secretary of State; the Charity Commissioners, for example, are appointed by the Home Secretary for England and Wales. They apply and interpret the law. They issue regulations or notes for guidance which supplement and add details to legislation. They have considerable discretion, and indeed it sometimes feels as though they make up the law as they go along.

They tend not to operate under the bright lights of public scrutiny, although they are accountable to their Secretary of State. Typically, they are backroom, backstairs organisations. Their characteristic styles are not to issue large public statements but either to make suggestions you cannot ignore or to pin you down with administrative darts. Some of them, like the Housing Corporation, also control funds – which adds to their operational power.

The watchdogs usually require bodies under their supervision to submit annual accounts and any amendments to their constitutions. They expect bodies to keep proper records and have some powers to investigate bodies which they suspect of slipping up. They may be able to prosecute for failing to comply with legislation; associations under the Registry of Friendly Societies, for example, are liable to prosecution if they fail to submit annual accounts.

Industrial relations legislation during the 1970s attempted to impose such a watchdog over trade unions. The Industrial Relations Act 1971 created a registrar of trade unions, to whom a trade union (which wished to be registered) had to submit rules and annual accounts, including statements of its objects, procedures for electing and removing members of its governing body, and procedures for disciplining members. The Trade Union and Labour Relations Acts 1974 and 1976 scaled this accountability down to the function of a certification officer, maintaining a list of trade unions, and requirements for annual returns and audited accounts.

Local authority expenditure is checked by an official appointed by the Secretary of State for the Environment known as the district auditor. He has power to disallow items of expenditure and apply to a court to order individual members and officials to repay unauthorised, improper expenditure themselves.

The Charities Act 1960 enables the Charity Commissioners in England and Wales to investigate a charity's affairs, to hold an enquiry and question officers, to remove and replace trustees for misconduct or mismanagement and to restrict its activities. Obviously with about 100,000 charities, many of which deal in few pounds at a time, the commissioners' supervision is not constant but, particularly if they have received a complaint, can be detailed and backed up by the Court of Chancery. They have suspended officers of a charity.[11]

They have warned charities about undertaking political activities (see 4.2). For example, in 1978 they put pressure on the charity War on Want over its involvement in human and legal rights projects and its publication of a politically provocative magazine. Its press statement captures the style:

We understand that, as a result of discussions (between the commissioners and the committee of War on Want), the committee has decided to abandon publication of *Poverty and Power* and to review certain projects, in the light of further consultation with the commissioners.[12]

4.2 THE LEGAL BASES OF ACTION

The law does not always have the same picture of the world as we do, and this is particularly so in respect of voluntary associations. To us the Fulham Association of Soup for Aristocrats may be a very real thing in our lives – we spend days and nights arguing over its actions and obey the resolutions of its executive committee. But a court of law might not be able to hold the association responsible for its actions.

The issue is that of 'legal personality' – does the body have an existence in law? is it an entity separate from its members?

People have 'legal personality' – they can sue and be sued, be tried in court, be held legally responsible for their actions. Bodies established by statute, including local authorities and limited companies, and by royal charter, including many universities, all have legal personalities. They are called corporate bodies or incorporated associations. It is possible, say, to sue a limited company for damages, or to go to a court for an injunction against a local authority undertaking some action, and so on. These bodies are seen in law as more than just the people who comprise the association; they are entities with an existence in their own right. An employee or a shareholder of a limited company can sue the company, or a ratepayer can sue a local authority.

UNINCORPORATED ASSOCIATIONS

But 'unincorporated associations', which include many voluntary associations, do not exist separately from their members. The Fulham Association of Soup for Aristocrats is no more than the collection of its members. You cannot sue the FASA, and conversely the FASA cannot sue. You can only sue as individuals the people who are responsible for running it.

The law's historical position on unincorporated associations has been that (a) the association had no separate existence from its members, and (b) the association consisted of a contract between its members. Thus, the rules of an association were a form of agreement between the members, not between the association as an entity and its members. So if you were chucked out of an association or the rules applied unfairly to you, it was just like being bitched at in a scratch game of cricket: the remedy was in your own hands – leave and take your bat and ball somewhere else.

These concepts ceased to work in respect of one kind of unincorporated association – trade unions. If a trade union chucked a guy out, he might not be able to work at his trade any more. If you thought a union's disciplinary action was unjust, was resigning your real remedy? So a number of cases in the courts established that a trade union could be dealt with in law as a corporate entity. Thus (a) its members could sue the union as an entity separate from themselves, and (b) someone expelled from or disciplined by a union could take it to court for a remedy. The

Trade Union and Labour Relations Acts 1974 and 1976 recognised such corporate aspects of unions.

It is difficult to assess whether other unincorporated associations will get caught up in a parallel development. Clearly we do attach much political and social significance to these associations, and, too, they are affected by the growth of legislation in social and welfare concerns, both for leisure and employment. However, we must recognise that the developments in trade union case-law were the courts' (and recently particularly Lord Denning's) response to the accumulation of legislation relating directly to trade unions. Moreover, the significance of trade unions in these judgements lies considerably in their exercise of judicial or administrative measures affecting people's rights not to be prevented from working. The legal position of most unincorporated associations continues to be markedly different from our political view of them.

The fact that unincorporated associations do not have legal personality means that they cannot sue or be sued or hold property. It means they cannot act except through the agency of their officers or authorised members. It means that the people running these associations are carrying legal responsibility individually for the association's affairs. When the FASA feeds lethal soup to a distressed aristocrat, the members of its management committee can expect to be held personally liable in law for any damages. Or if the FASA gets into debt they may have to pay up out of their own pockets. They are trustees for its affairs.

A voluntary association, say, a parent–teacher association runs a fund-raising fete. Somebody cuts their face on a broken goldfish bowl; the members of the executive committee individually are sued for damages; the case against them is successful; they have to pay the damages with their own money. Strictly speaking, they could not even use the funds raised at the fete for this, but if they could show they had acted prudently they might be allowed by the court to put the PTA's funds towards the damages. (It is possible and wise to insure against such eventualities, of course.)

TRUSTEES

There are two kinds of trusteeship: the personal responsibility, which I have just described, for the affairs of an unincorporated association; responsibility for buildings and land. In both cases it involves an individual responsibility for collective business. The group or the association is not responsible as an entity; a few of its members take this responsibility personally.[13]

Suppose the PTA fete (above) is successful, the members of the executive committee are – again, individually – responsible for spending it on the purposes for which it was raised. The fete is to raise funds for a minibus for the school, but after the cash has been collected the executive receive an appeal for a famine and argue 'If we bought a second-hand minibus, we could send £500 of this money to the famine relief, and really how can we stand by with children starving . . .'. They are then liable to have to pay the £500 out of their own pockets. They are trustees for the money which they raised.

An important – and sometimes surprising – implication of this personal trusteeship is that it does not allow us to pass on money unless we have made sure that it is to be applied to the purposes for which the funds were raised. That PTA should not hand over the cash to another body such as, say, a local authority school transport fund without ensuring that it is to be properly spent on the school minibus. Its members cannot free themselves of their responsibility. Similarly we cannot delegate functions to other bodies unless it is an effective discharge of our trusteeship. This means that in setting up subcommittees we cannot allow them freedom to commit expenditure as they decide unless we supervise it in keeping with this responsibility.

Trusteeship for lands and buildings is different. In the above instance, all the members of the current management or executive committee are responsible. However, a body, such as this, whose membership changes continually cannot own buildings or land. Therefore, an unincorporated association needs another way of owning property. It appoints a small number of people – often, three – as trustees. The property is vested in them, and they take personal responsibility as trustees for it. When all the chips are down, it is their responsibility to deploy it for the purposes for which it was acquired.

Some bodies, notably some charities, are established as trusts under a 'trust deed'. Named individuals are made responsible for all the bodies' affairs, rather than, as above, executive committees elected by a membership.

Beyond the simple signposts which I am offering, trust law is extraordinarily complex, having grown from mediaeval efforts at tax avoidance and now encompassing not only our voluntary, unincorporated associations but also investment bodies and the devices which the rich use to skip over death duties and taxes. But, if it sounds crudely speaking as though a few people are carrying a millstone round their necks for the rest of us, that's how it is.

CHARITABLE STATUS

The achievement of charitable status does not affect the above discussion about the legal personality of an association. A charity might be an unincorporated association or a corporate body of some form.[14] The advantages of being a charity are:

– relief on taxes and rates;
– opportunity to receive grants from other charities;

Plus a certain cachet on the good works scene.

To be a charity an association must have charitable objects. In most cases charities are registered with the Charity Commissioners and supervised by them (in Scotland by the Secretary of State for Scotland) but it is possible to be considered charitable by the Inland Revenue without being registered.

Charitable objects were defined by Lord Macnaghten in the House of Lords in 1891:

> . . . trusts for the relief of poverty; trusts for the advancement of education; trusts for the advancement of religion; and trusts for other purposes beneficial to the community.

The – still relevant – legal foundation is the preamble to the Charitable Uses Act 1601, which lists charitable purposes:

> . . . some for relief of aged, impotent, and poor people, some for maintenance of sick and maimed soldiers and mariners, schools of learning, free schools, and scholars in universities: some for repair of bridges, ports, havens, causeways, churches, seabanks and highways; some for education and preferment of orphans; some for or towards the relief, stock or maintenance for houses of correction; some for marriages for poor maids; some for the supportation, aid and help of young tradesmen,

handicraftsmen, and persons decayed; and others for relief or redemption of prisoners or captives, and for aid or ease of any poor inhabitants concerning payment of fifteens, setting out of soldiers, and other taxes.

Perhaps it shows the problematic nature of charity in our society that this list has never been superseded and is always quoted as the basic text. Do the objects of an association fit this list? An association for marrying impotent men to poor maids looks a winner, especially if they could maintain a house of correction.

Whether an association can be considered charitable is a matter for some nice legal judgements. Does it benefit the community or a section, and is that section fitting for charity along the lines of the 1601 list? Courts have found that a trust to promote Delius' music to be charitable but not George Bernard Shaw's legacy to have *Androcles and the Lion* translated into a 40-letter alphabet.[15]

One rule is definite: charities cannot engage in political activities. But this is not easy to interpret. When, for example, does 'education' become political persuasion? Charities have been warned off overt campaigning by the Charity Commissioners.[16] Nonetheless, a charity might manage to campaign on a conservative cause. The Charity Commissioners would not regard the straightforward presentation of a case to, say, the Government as a breach of charitable objects so long as this did not become the main purpose of an association.[17]

Another definite rule is that charities may not be controlled by the people who benefit from them. In the strictest interpretation people who are employed by or helped by a charity cannot sit on its governing body, its executive committee. Charity is conceived as what some – rich – people do for other – poor – people, rather than self-help. This clashes with attempts to build democratic bodies in which the people who are the objects of the charity move into control of their lives and share in or take over the running of the charity. Fundamentally, charity is modelled on the soup kitchen. However, some charities do include small-scale representation of people who benefit from them.

Charity law has accumulated through case-law on the 1601 foundation. Attempts to review and codify it into a coherent body of law have failed. The Charities Act 1960 achieved some rationalisation but the Goodman Committee in 1976 could do no better than the status quo. In practice, much depends on the interpretation of the law by the Charity Commissioners (see 4.1).

ULTRA VIRES

The phrase is magic. It can stop a committee in its tracks; it can reduce hard men to stuttering rage.

The basic concept is straightforward. A body can only do what it has been set up to do, can only act within its powers. Any other action is 'outside its powers', or in Latin 'ultra vires', and is not allowed. A neat example is of a company which was established to provide information and facilities for visitors to the Festival of Britain 1951. When it turned its business to breeding pigs, a court held that it was ultra vires to borrow money for that.[18]

The background is that bodies such as local authorities, limited companies and associations are only allowed to do what the law (or their own legal basis, their constitution) says they can do. This contrasts with the freedom of individuals under the law to do anything except what the law says they cannot do. Thus, a local authority can only act in ways provided for in acts of parliament. A limited company can only do what its memorandum of association says are its objects. An association can only perform the functions written into its constitution.

The most common grounds for an action being ultra vires are that, as above, the association is doing something that is not provided for by the law or its constitution. The Fulham Association of Soup for Aristocrats has not been established to serve caviare in Fulham or soup in Solihull. An action can also be ultra vires because it is done by the wrong person or body within an organisation, if the body has not been properly constituted or exceeds its powers. Thus, if a subcommittee carries out functions that have not under the constitution (or law or rules) been delegated to it the actions may be ultra vires.

If an ultra vires action is proposed, a court could grant an injunction to prevent it. If an action is ultra vires, the people who have incurred the expenditure could be held personally responsible for paying it themselves.

The application of the doctrine of ultra vires is not simple. The fineness of the distinction is illustrated by two of the fundamental cases, both of which concerned companies in the railway business in the nineteenth century. One company which had been established to make and sell railway equipment was held to be ultra vires in purchasing a concession to construct a railway in

Belgium. However, another company which ran railways was held not to be ultra vires in letting workshops in the arches under railway bridges.[19] In the latter case Lord Selbourne made a historic judgement:

> The ultra vires rule ought to be reasonably, and not unreasonably, understood and applied, and whatsoever may fairly be regarded as incidental to or consequential upon those things which the legislature has authorised, ought not (unless expressly prohibited) to be held, by judicial construction, to be ultra vires.

That, of course, is sensible but it and subsequent case-law do not make it any easier for the layman to tell what would be ultra vires except in fairly obvious cases.

It is not terribly helpful to look now to company law, which has developed its own course; it is easy enough to write objects that enable the company to engage in a broad range of activities. The application of the doctrine of ultra vires to local authorities is more rigorous: a local authority has to be able to show there is statutory authority for all its actions; the district auditor (see 4.1) can apply for a court order that members and staff who have incurred ultra vires expenditure must repay it out of their own pockets.

But there must be doubts how a court would handle an unincorporated association. Where money or property is involved a court could act if a member or an interested party brought a case. But where no loss was concerned a court might have difficulty establishing whether anything ultra vires had happened, indeed whether legally anything had happened at all.

The most effective bodies in dealing with ultra vires are the public watchdogs. The Charity Commissioners are likely to take a firm line on ultra vires actions, particularly if the actions take the association beyond its constitutional charitable objects. Thus, cases tend to go no further than debate within associations or stern warnings from the Charity Commissioners and are not put to the ultimate test of the courts.

4.3 CONSTRAINTS ON MEETING, TALKING AND MAKING MONEY

In this section I indicate some major points where, when we are involved in meetings and committees, we need to be on our guard. Again, these are brief signposts, and I re-emphasise the caution required in applying them to particular cases. A court's judgement will depend both on more detailed interpretation of the law and on the circumstances of the particular case.

As I said in Chapter 4.1, the starting-point is that in Britain we (as individuals) are free under the law to do anything except what the law prevents us from doing. There is not a bill of rights or a statement of our constitutional freedoms, such as provide the basic script for the final reel of so many old American movies. In this country we are free to do anything . . . except that through acts of parliament, common law and EEC law we are surrounded by limits on our freedom in order to protect other people's freedom and property and to maintain the power of the state. These limits are not codified and thus overlap, criss-cross, leave tiny gaps to slip through, clobber you with the swing if you escape the roundabout etc.

MEETINGS

Restrictions apply to the places where you can hold meetings. Use of local authority buildings and open space is subject to its bye-laws and local acts of parliament which may set conditions for lettings, notice of meetings etc. Meetings are subject to law about trespass (I indicated in Chapter 3.12 how this could work to the advantage of the organisers).

Meetings and marches are subject to law about obstructing the highways, police powers to regulate traffic, pedestrians and processions, temporary bans (by local authorities with the consent of the Secretary of State) on all processions in an area, and committing a public nuisance.

There are a number of rather generalised acts of parliament and aspects of common law which restrict what can happen in meetings. They are subject to the Public Meeting Act 1908 and Public Order Act 1936, including the offence of trying to break up a public meeting (see 3.12). The police have a duty in common law to prevent a breach of the peace (see 3.12). Meetings could also be treated as 'unlawful assemblies' on two grounds: that three or more persons meet for an illegal purpose; or that they endanger public peace or put firm and courageous persons in the neighbourhood in fear. Meetings are also unlawful if they are defined as 'rout' or 'riot'. And, even if these stages are not reached, the police may charge people with resisting or wilfully obstructing a policeman in the execution of his duty which could encompass a wide range of activities.

More specific legislation relating to the content of meetings includes the Race Relations Act 1967, Prevention of Terrorism Act 1976 and Incitement to Disaffection Act 1934.

Thus, much discretion lies with the police and the courts: do the police decide to go in and break the meeting up?; do the courts return 'guilty' verdicts on those whom the police charge? This discretion is affected by the political climate: has the time come to draw the line?; can we extend the boundaries of the High Court's vision of democracy?

This realisation suggests either despair or cynicism – either the application of the law is an ineffectual liberal response to the impending tyranny or it is the actual tyranny's response to our friends and allies. But, given the uncertainty and political context of the law, the fundamental rights to hold meetings have been established in law, and we keep re-asserting them.

ASSOCIATION

Likewise, the starting-point is the freedom to associate and to form associations to protect ourselves, our workmates and colleagues, and our friends. This is limited mainly by the laws about conspiracy, which are notoriously subject to political fluctuations. Conspiracy is an agreement – written, verbal or just 'a nod or a wink' – to commit a criminal offence (Criminal Law Act 1977), to corrupt public morals or to outrage public decency. The action does not have to be actually carried out; indeed, the connection between the people and some illegal act can be tenuous. Consider: trade unions were sometimes seen as conspiracies until the Trade Union Act 1871.

DEFAMATION

Freedom of speech is restricted by the possibilities of being sued for libel or slander. Libel applies to permanent forms of expression, such as newspapers, magazines, books, TV and radio. Slander applies mostly only to the spoken word. To the offender libel feels more dangerous than slander: the evidence is easier to pin down; and the success of the case does not depend, as slander mostly does, on proving some financial loss as a result of the statement.[20]

Defamation broadly speaking is a statement which would tend to lower someone in the estimation of right-thinking members of society or cause them to shun or avoid them by attacking his or her reputation or character. It applies to individuals, not groups or classes.[21] It can be accidental: in a classic case a newspaper writer invented 'Artemus Jones' and was sued successfully by a real Artemus Jones; in another classic a newspaper's picture caption of a man and woman whose engagement was said to have been announced led to a successful case by the man's wife. If someone could show that one of the – fictional – examples which I have used in this book is identified as him and defames him, I could be in trouble.

Cases of libel or slander are brought by the person who believes himself defamed against those who speak, write, publish or disseminate the statements. The case can be brought against someone who sells a publication or who repeats someone else's statement as well as he who originated it. The person who brings the case seeks damages, money to recompense for the loss of character or reputation.

The main defences against an action for libel or slander are: fair comment; justification; privilege.

'Fair comment' is opinion or comment honestly made, without malice and believed to be true upon matters of public interest. The defence of 'justification' applies to facts, not comment, and the defendant must prove that the statement was true. It would not be wise to assume that because what you have said about Algernon is true that you cannot be done for defamation. A further defence is that the defamation was perpetrated innocently and that an offer of amends was made but refused.

Privilege can be 'absolute' or 'qualified'. Absolute privilege enables MPs in the House of Commons and judges in the courts to say anything however inaccurate or damaging without being sued for libel. Qualified privilege is a defence where:

– a statement made in pursuance of a legal, social or moral duty to persons who have a corresponding interest in hearing the statements. This covers communications between persons possessing a common interest, for example, between employer

and employee, and statements made in good faith by a member of a public body in pursuance of his duties;
– agenda of local authorities and other bodies under the Public Bodies (Admission to Meetings) Act 1960;
– fair and accurate reports in the press of public meetings or meetings of local authorities and public bodies (though the defendant should be willing to publish a letter of explanation from someone claiming to be libelled), and of government and official documents.

How far 'qualified privilege' could be applied to our concerns in committees and meetings is uncertain. It has been upheld as a defence for a statement made in a local council meeting,[22] but you could not rely on it for the non-statutory representative bodies. Perhaps we should set up a test-case. . . .

FUND-RAISING

For voluntary associations, particularly community organisations and clubs, this is a sensitive topic. Not only is raising funds rather necessary, but everyone is so friendly that it can be difficult to do exactly what the law requires. In fact, fund-raising is more regulated by the law than you would guess from your average bazaar or gala day.

Collecting money in the street or house-to-house requires a licence from the local police authority and stringent conditions are applied; it is not easy to get a licence. (This also applies to selling goods with a charitable object.) However, the local chief of police can give an exemption for house-to-house collections on a small, local scale.

Lotteries are controlled by the Betting, Gaming and Lotteries Act 1963 and the Lotteries Act 1975. Permission is not required for small lotteries which are subsidiary to an entertainment or for private lotteries. A small lottery, which is conducted entirely at the place of the entertainment and is not its main purpose, is limited to prizes which cost up to £50, with no cash prizes. A private lottery is only for members of an association, and tickets must not be sold to other people. Small and private lotteries must devote their funds, after deduction of limited expenses and giving prizes, to, respectively, purposes other than private gain or to the objects of the society. Societies which run larger lotteries selling tickets to the public other than at the place of the entertainment have to be registered with the local authority, and conditions are set about prize-money, expenses and conditions of sale.

Associations should also be circumspect about fund-raising through trading. If they are not charitable, they are, for all their good intentions, liable to tax. Charities are generally considered safe in this respect so long as the trading activities are clearly subsidiary and a means to the charitable objects. If the trading takes precedence, they face losing their charitable status.

I noted in Chapter 4.2 the importance of recognising responsibilities for funds which have been raised. Remember, too, that well-meaning chaps in voluntary associations are not exempt from criminal law in respect of fraud, falsifying the accounts etc.

NOTES

1. *The Guardian* 14 November 1978.
2. These notes refer to English law; the processes are different in Scottish law.
3. Lord Wilberforce in Heatons Transport v TGWU (1973).
4. Salt and Others v National Graphical Association, *The Times* 16 May 1978.
5. *The Times* 26 January 1978.
6. See Perrins and Jeffreys (1970), pp. 156–7.
7. Lord Russell Carruth v ICI Ltd (1937): 'There are many matters relating to the conduct of a meeting which lie entirely in the hands of those people who are present and constitute the meeting. . . . If necessary a vote must be taken to ascertain the wishes of the majority.'
8. Lord Cranworth in Forbes v Eden (1867) quoted in Josling and Alexander (1975), p. 34.
9. *The Times* 26 January 1978.
10. *The Guardian* 28 October 1977.
11. See Nightingale (1973), p. 278 onward.
12. *The Guardian* 10 November 1978.
13. There can be no one simple statement of legal liability which can be applied to all circumstances. In different situations the nominated trustees, the members of committee and the members themselves may be held responsible. See Josling and Alexander (1975), pp. 102–17.
14. Corporate status may be achieved by establishment under the Companies Acts or the Industrial and Provident Societies Acts. Some comparable features can be achieved by registration under the Friendly Societies Act 1974.
15. Quoted in Nightingale (1973), p. 37.

16. See Nightingale (1973), p. 45 onward.
17. See Stevenson (1972), p. 56 onward.
18. Re Introductions Ltd (1968), quoted in Perrins and Jeffreys (1970), p. 44.
19. Ashbury Railway Carriage Co Ltd v Riche (1875) and Attorney General v Great Eastern Railway (1880), quoted in Perrins and Jeffreys (1970), p. 44.
20. Slander can apply not only to statements which lead to some financial loss but also to damaging statements about a lack of chastity or a contagious disease.
21. But if the alleged defamation is against a class or group which is small and well-defined, it may be actionable.
22. Horrocks v Lowe (1975) quoted in Wade and Phillips (1977), p. 467.

5 Action

5.1 PEOPLE

Here we all are. The meeting is about to begin. Our minds and
pencils are sharp. Dolly is competent at chairing. Jo has got the
paperwork in order. Winston has learnt all about security alarms
for the discussion of item 6 on the agenda. Reg has tanked up to
give himself courage to say what he really thinks this time. Nigel
feels the paranoia setting in. What will make this an effective
meeting?

An answer which comes quickly to many minds is: 'No power
on earth'. Suspicions about the effectiveness of committees and
formal meetings are common: 'This democracy is all very well but
it takes time'; 'All you ever get out of a committee is a shabby
compromise'; 'Talk, talk, talk and nothing decided again'. To
some extent these comments indicate ideological differences or
fundamental misgivings about the benefits of collective action in
any circumstances. But they do point to problems which even the
wildest evangelists for committee power have to cope with.

There are no magic formulae, no certain prescriptions to make
committees and meetings work. Obviously I think that we can
make a lot of progress by following the rules and conventions for
conducting meetings which I have discussed in Chapters 2 and 3.
On top of that, a combination of interpersonal skills, tactics,
manoeuvres and animal cunning can make it more or less likely
that we have effective meetings. In this final chapter I put forward
some ideas of this kind. I do not promise they will work.
Associations operate in different circumstances and have different people and skills available.

INVOLVEMENT

I write in the naive assumption that you are seeking to involve
people, though some committees work nicely with a sound chair,

a dynamic secretary and a circle of tailor's dummies.

One problem is that to apply the rules of procedure strictly often turns people off. To get people involved it is sometimes necessary to relax, even to be rather loose in a style that horrifies people who know how a meeting *should* be conducted.

Some devices which people running meetings can try:

- wander around the topic for a while, let people ramble on about slightly irrelevant issues if it helps them focus on the topic and gives them confidence to speak;
- go round the room person-by-person (assuming it is not too big) or find and pose the questions which everyone jumps to answer (once someone has spoken they are more likely to speak again);
- let discussions occasionally go on beyond the point of decision because often it's only as the debate tails off that a new or shy person breaks in;
- encourage contributions from the floor by writing up ideas on a blackboard or huge sheet of paper;
- think about the arrangement of chairs and tables (sitting in a circle encourages more informal participation than in rows, lining up the officers behind a table on a platform sets them apart from the members, etc.);
- talk about 'real things', the nitty-gritty, not just 'the major issues';
- be clear about the subject, recap on past discussions, spell out the facts and implications, make the main points stand out;
- don't keep referring to other organisations by initials and to people without saying who they are (so I went to see Jeremy at FUBWA and Frankie from DIPO dropped in with Colin.' Laughter. What's funny?).

See also Chapter 2.2 on chairing.

However, although such devices can involve some people in discussions, unless you move into an orderly, decision-taking style, you are liable to lose others. Even those who've enjoyed the chat may not see the point of coming again.

TASKS AND ROLES

Consider the tasks involved in running a committee and association: lobbying; speaking in public; leading delegations; putting on and controlling a public meeting; writing letters; keeping the books; developing the strategy; keeping sights on the wider philosophical and political implications; devising the tactics; infighting; organising retreat with dignity; conciliating; chatting up philanthropists; understanding the Manpower Services Commission; filling in forms; researching facts and figures; keeping the group together; caring about the law; not caring about the law; having a conscience; speaking up for the outsiders; applying expert knowledge; managing thousands of pounds; taking care of the pence; interviewing staff; cutting stencils; designing posters; carrying banners; storming the barricades; etc.

Organisations place different priorities on these jobs and have different supplies of people willing to undertake them. This means:

— there are many different ways of involving people;
— you need to consider not just the individual characteristics of who should fill the positions of officers but how you get the necessary range of skills into the committee and the whole association.

As a starting point look at some contrasting roles that an association may need filled:

— publicist	— backroom worker;
— knocker on doors	— paperworker;
— charismatic leader	— conciliator;
— winner	— conscience;
— cynic	— innovator;
— elitist expert	— voice of the masses;
— visionary	— tactician;
— strategist	— day-to-day problem solver.

Any one person can only fill a few of these roles. Is it possible to go all out to win and have conscientious doubts? Maybe your 'winner' could also be your 'paperworker' and/or your 'tactician'.

Most organisations need a few broad basic types of person around:

— someone who cares intensely about the main purpose, someone with fire in the belly and/or intellectual conviction;

—someone who holds people together, performs group maintenance, provides community glue;
—someone who slogs through the boring work, volunteers for
muckshifting;
—someone who acts as a conscience about law, money and
constitution.

You also need people who know about the subject or issues you
are involved in.

These are not fixed categories; I offer them to provoke thoughts
about the range of tasks you need to get performed and the range
of people you have available to fill them. For example, I prefer to
chair a meeting than be an ordinary member – at least as chair I
know where I am, feel significant and do not need many
convictions – whereas someone who can really argue a case is
wasted as the chair. Remember that some people are good in
meetings but not outside them and vice versa. Some people are
fantastic at declaring in public what ought to be done but never
deliver the work. Some people never open their mouths in a
meeting but slog away night-after-night addressing envelopes.
And many people only get really involved when they have some
work to do.

Consider also:

—that people may act differently in a formal role than they do
privately and, for example, a treasurer may be very conscientious about an association's finances but hopeless with his own
housekeeping;
—that people may act differently in different groups, and someone
who is a responsible chair in one committee may be a wild
backbench rebel in another (and not just because of different
policies);
—that groups tend to sort people out to cover the various roles.

People within a group tend to adapt to fill the different roles that
enable them to get along with each other and make the group
work. Someone grows into being the secretary. We modify our
actions so that there is space for our ally's point of view. We may
become the mouthpiece for, say, radical opinions because
otherwise that point of view is lost or we have nothing to
contribute.

But we can get stuck in roles within a group – everyone else expects us to act in a predictable way. If our ally Winston who is normally forceful and talkative stays quiet, the rest of us are confused and even begin to think we must be saying the wrong things. In a small meeting we thrash around looking for the way of drawing him in, for the right things to say. If Dolly who usually makes the decisive points which wrap up discussions is missing, the chair may find that discussions do not flow to an end as easily. Or if it is usually Cressida who 'goes over the top', when she is absent it can be difficult for other members to initiate the discussion, and items may pass on the nod which would otherwise be long and furiously debated.

The fact that we have sorted out our roles and get on with each other does not necessarily mean we are doing the right thing. We are having friendly chats over a glass of wine rather than facing up to the unpleasant argument about controlling expenditure. We are boosting each other's egos rather than work out how to make the case to the public.

So often the problem, particularly in voluntary associations, is the level of involvement of a few people as compared to the rest. Three or four of us know what it is all about, get on together, nobly slog through the work. And the rest of them are, we think, apathetic; or good people but they're busy, got families to bring up, time-consuming real jobs, more rose-bushes than I care to count. So I'll write the report, and I'll come with you to the lawyers because I understand the contract, and I write minutes best and really it's no trouble, and I can design posters, and I'm an expert on leases, and if I'm going to be this involved I ought to sit on finance subcommittee, and now you've buggered up the public consultations I'm going to have to sort out the trouble at the mosque. And the secret of power is so often just being there – look what happened while I was on holiday – that to carry through my line I've got to be at this meeting and that subcommittee and check out the liaison committee in case anything crops up. The outcomes include:

- the others can't enter the discussions at the same level of knowledge so they just approve everything I do;
- the others lose interest and drift off;
- I can't cope, start missing meetings, and suddenly everyone knows I'm an opportunist;

— I wake up one morning, ask 'What is the meaning of life?' and
  resign from everything, leaving the others in the lurch.

It is not easy to overcome this. Work tends to land in the laps of
those with already enough to do; positions go to people who are
already trusted because of what they are doing somewhere else;
there are networks of committees and meetings, one meeting leads
to another, one committee to representing it on another committee. None of us really trust more than a very few, if any, other
people to do things as well as we could do them ourselves. We find
our allies and stick with them.
  But I think there is a law about committees and meetings:

— people get involved as a consequence of doing some work, or of
  perceiving that they have an effect on what happens.

This is the opposite of the usual comments

  The others don't seem bothered;
  The rest of the committee don't seem committed enough for us
  to expect them to do this work.

In other words, we shouldn't sit around waiting for the others to
show interest. We should dish out the jobs to people and watch
(some of) them become more involved. But it's difficult and can
take longer to explain a job than do it yourself; it's an act of faith;
and it's less power for you and me.
  When people do get involved we must keep using them — even if
it means an extra phone call — and keep consulting them — even if
we think we know what they'll say.

KEEPING GOING

To be effective in meetings, we need to maintain the organisation
outside the meetings.

Communications
If all members just turn up cold at meetings, it is unlikely that they
will operate effectively. At least two or three people need to have
talked about what is coming up — clarified issues, sorted out who
says what, fixed the interaction.

In highly politically structured organisations, like local authorities, this is achieved by caucus meetings of political parties. The Labour and Conservative councillors meet separately to decide their line on issues – this can be the scene of the liveliest debates and most naked power. Allies need to meet; it is hard to dominate a meeting together just by raised eyebrows, passing tightly-folded notes and extra-sensory perception. Plot: I will open by saying . . . ; the main issues for us are . . . ; we'll probe their strength by putting up an amendment . . . ; you can sacrifice yourself . . . .

Talk, too, to people who aren't your undying allies. A problem sprung on someone in a meeting can mean they take up a hard, defensive position that even they can't find a way out of later. Soften them up or do a deal before the meeting; just informing them gives them a chance to calm down or think through a constructive line. Nothing wrecks meetings like people who think they have been kept in the dark deliberately (except *perhaps* people to whom you have intentionally given false information).

Many canny politicians, however, value the chance of catching their opponents by surprise and without their allies. I reckon you need to be very clever and powerful to win more than the most temporary advantage out of this. You need either to achieve an irrevocable, impregnable position by it or to have the strength to smash your opponents even harder when they get up to complain. Your average conspirator, particularly in committees without entrenched political lines, is simply stacking up enmity for future meetings.

Good communications for a committee means being able to reach people on the phone, at work, in the pub or wherever you meet for everyday reasons. Tell them about any big issues or incidents between meetings particularly if anyway they will read about it in the press or hear it from someone else in the pub. Nothing creates a fuss like a dignitary who thinks he has been forgotten.

Many organisations circulate newsletters, journals, newspapers, wallsheets, etc., but these are beyond the scope of this book.

Jobs
Be definite about who is doing what and by when. Set deadlines. Don't rely on friendship and honest eyes.

Never say 'We'll fix a meeting when we've finished the report'. Fix the date of the meeting so it acts as a deadline.

Size of committees

For reasons I have never understood this is often considered a major issue. Recommendations have been made that no executive body should have more than nine members (Nathan Report), or a school governing body 24 members 'maximum for efficient operation' (Taylor Report, p. 24). I don't think it matters that much, and it depends on what kind of committee you want. In a politically divided group it is more important to get the representation of people and interests right than to worry about whether 12 or 18 or 24 or 37 is an effective size. But a likeminded group of activists who want to work very closely together may be effective with only half-a-dozen.

Staff or workers

The relationship between committees and paid officials, if any, is bound to be occasionally, if not always, problematic. The principle is clear: the committee makes decisions and the officials carry them out within instructions or delegated powers (see 3.10 and 5.2). But inevitably staff have a great say in what actually happens. They do the job full-time (or so they say); they may be professional experts; they implement decisions, and in doing so adapt them to the circumstances. Even in terms of responding to political pressures, an elected member of a committee – a councillor, for example – may be less aware of demands and needs than the official who deals directly with the people. A party machine can keep out the daylight just as much as an official bureaucracy.

5.2 DECISIONS

A major difficulty is that meetings are at fixed points in a fluid situation. Events don't fall into place a day or two before meetings so that we can make tidy decisions. Sod's Law dictates that the critical events take place a couple of days later, making our decision look stupid. Or the long-simmering row boils over ten days before the meeting, even though we have the issue on the agenda to resolve.

How can we cope with this? How can we take good decisions? I suggest, following the points in Chapter 1, that 'good decisions' have several characteristics:

1. *They are accepted as legitimate.* People and other bodies accept the decision as one which the meeting is entitled to make. They therefore support or recognise or obey or tolerate it or treat it as a basis for negotiation. They may fight the decision but they accept that the meeting was within its rights in making it.

2. *They make things happen.* The decision creates some action – even if only standing still or deliberate delay, even if only asking for a further report.

3. *They are well considered and well advised.* The pious words in Chapter 1.3 about sharing knowledge and skills and about open criticism have been put into effect. The meeting has thought about what officers, members, representatives, workers or available experts have to say.

4. *They fit the best available facts.* Facts are never perfect and tend to change, but the ones in front of us are as accurate as we get them in the time and realities of the situation.

5. *They fit the situation.* Such intangibles as the political climate, the mood of the membership and the character of the other side have been taken into account. The fluidity of the situation has been recognised, as has the Nth dimension of the personalities involved. (This is not simply a good decision; it is a miracle.)

6. *They are consistent with policies or precedents.* We have objectives, guidelines or a statement of our direction. We have precedents established about our line and style. The decision should be consistent with these, or, if not, we should recognise the change in direction and its implications.

7. *They are consistent with the resources available.* The cash – the people – the equipment – we can only work within these capabilities, of course.

8. *They are timed rightly.* One kind of action is right to start a campaign; another to climax it. Or, a paper which is to be fed into a cycle of local authority committees may need to be approved months before any action is required. Committees have often to make decisions before they are really pressing (see 3.3).

9. *They are made at the appropriate level.* Different associations require different levels and details of decisions. The executive committee of a local pressure group may need to make and record decisions about who is to carry the left-hand pole of the banner.

The executive committee of a national charity may need only to approve the director's report – 'Carry on the good work. Time for sherry'. Between such extremes, committees formulate policy in broad outline or specify actions in various degrees of detail.

What enables these 'good decisions to be made'?

INFORMATION AND INSTRUCTION

First, the meeting is, as this book has described, properly conducted. The formal procedure of agenda, rules of debate, motions and amendments establishes a structure – applied as magnanimously and as correctly as appropriate – for tackling complex business in a fair and orderly manner. The authority of the chair helps shape discussions, coax the meeting towards decisions and ensure that the decision is clearly stated.

Secondly, and this is my subject here, the meeting should be the master – intellectually and politically – of its input and its output. The input is the information which it needs to come to a decision; the output is the statement of how it intends to act. The meeting has to control not only its own internal process but the external process – what happens outside it – before and after. In traditional committee procedure this process is conceived as

– *receiving* information on what has happened, and
– *instructing* what will happen.

The words 'receiving' in connection with reports and 'instructing' on actions sound old-fashioned and bureaucratic but they summarise the concepts even if most meetings are looser.

Receiving reports
A meeting has two sources of information:

– the speeches or contributions of members;
– the reports of committees or subcommittees, officers, delegations, working parties etc.

From the perspective of the people running the meeting, the first are unpredictable and probably partisan. You can't rely on them to present the facts and issues which are needed for good decisions. You have to ensure the meeting receives them through reports. (I am not talking about formal debates on motions where it is up to the proposer and seconder to out their own case, and to their allies and opponents to present theirs.)

Reports can take different forms: investigations by special committees, working parties or officers as instructed at previous meetings; regular reports from standing committees and officers – the report of the treasurer or bar subcommittee, or the headteacher's report to a school governing body; and some have been specially prepared by officers or members to meet needs which have arisen since a previous meeting. Reports may be briefing papers or may argue for a particular recommendation. Some meetings scarcely open their mouths without a report on the table, whilst in other bodies the presentation of a report represents a rare outbreak of thoroughness.

It is handling reports that defeats many meetings. Even if there is a report, it only approximately covers the topic. If it is a written report, members have not read it beforehand. If it is verbal, they daydream through. Then the discussion shoots off all over the place, sometimes going over again what is in the report, sometimes ignoring it. The decision seems to get the feel of the meeting at the time but later everyone realises that nothing has actually been resolved. We send up a few prayers that things will fall into place somehow and make for the pub. After all, we can have another crack at it at the next meeting.

Given my ideas of 'good decisions', a report should:

– begin by stating its starting-point (the problem which it is tackling, or the terms of reference or instruction given to it);
– be founded on the best available facts;
– analyse the issues and appraise the situation;
– set out the implications for policies and precedents;
– set out the constraints, including resources (how much does it cost?).

The analysis and appraisal of the situation includes the themes behind the facts and/or the implications of different courses of action and/or likely reactions from other bodies. How it is written depends on the kind of body to which the report is being made. A subcommittee report to a pressure group's executive might discuss the possible reactions of the local council in lit-up political language. An officer's report to a local authority committee is not expected to get into politics: never '. . . and this proposal will really make the Labour Party hopping mad . . .' though perhaps '. . . Members may wish to consider the implications of this proposal in the light of the authority's comprehensive schools policies'.

In a good report the meeting has the information required for a decision on a particular topic. The writers must therefore not only collect information and sort out issues but think about how the discussion might develop. The meeting can:

– receive the report (or refer it back);
– approve its recommendations (or amend them or not approve them) (see 3.10).

Therefore the report should be neutral and comprehensive enough to enable different actions to be assessed by its readers. Even if it strongly recommends one action, it should not obscure other possibilities.

Instructing action

Most of what a meeting wants done cannot actually be done by the meeting. The secretary will have to write a letter. The chair will have to negotiate with the other side. A subcommittee will have to investigate further. A deputation will have to argue the case with the council. The chief education officer will have to implement the resolution to, say, abolish corporal punishment in schools. What the meeting actually does is to instruct or authorise action.

This instruction should:

– be clear so there can be no mistaking intentions;
– state who will do what, when and how;
– be specific about what should be done (but not necessarily spell it out in detail).

But a meeting often goes, with disastrous consequences

Oh well, I'm sure Dolly can sort it out, and we wouldn't want to tie her hands

or

Resolved: subject to agreement with the community, the rock

band that Cressida's flatmate's friend plays in be asked to perform at the *Babylon for Beginners* evening next week.

Different levels of detail in the instruction are appropriate to different bodies. In one pressure group everything may be done in committee meetings down to settling who is going to collect whom in whose car. Someone drafts a policy statement for the next meeting but the meeting goes over the statement in minute detail, maybe arguing over commas. Outside the meeting the chair or spokesperson is authorised to talk to the press or a small number of members forms a deputation to the local authority, but they have little freedom of action. In another pressure group, however, the chair and a couple of committee-members may be so dominant that they carry on as they like, and meetings are a charade to approve their actions.

The level of detail depends on the strength of the association – whether it is a body which ploughs on regardless or whether any movement at all requires a lot of stick. It depends how much you trust each other. It depends on how you will refer back to the minutes at future meetings. It depends on the delicacy of the task – you can't spell out the points on which you are prepared to give way in a negotiation if the other side will read your minutes before you meet them. But the instruction, either actually in the resolution or in the debate leading up to it, must be clear about the constraints upon the action – the points at which further authorisation is needed and the limits on expenditure.

A good basis for formulating a clear instruction is to have a good report to work on. The report may actually provide a recommendation which can be adopted or amended. It should anyway clarify and structure the discussion, separating out the issues so that the decisions which follow from different thoughts can be spotted quickly. A strong report often leads a meeting by the nose to a decision.

Uses and abuses
So this is one process which makes it more likely that a meeting will be effective. If a problem arises that cannot be resolved there and then, rather than kick it around inconclusively and rush to a patched-up decision, you instruct an officer, official, a subcommittee or a working party to investigate and report back. It does so to the – probably – next meeting, and its report and recom

mendations either are approved and put directly into action or at least provide something tangible that can be modified to your requirements.

The first abuse of this process is that you never actually discuss anything in a meeting – local authorities have perfected this. Something crops up, you put it back to another meeting for a report, the report appears, and you rubber-stamp its recommendation. You don't think; you never worry. You become slaves of the expert members and officers who plod away on working parties or burn the midnight oil to prepare reports.

The second abuse is that you shift issues away from the public gaze into the recesses of the organisation which you control. The full meeting is a random lot of bolshie individuals, but Bar Subcommittee, say, is a likeminded bunch of specialists in awe of (a) the treasurer and (b) the steward and his disinterested professional advice.

Whereas these two abuses can be efficient methods of avoiding controversy, a third abuse tends to bring the ceiling down round your ears. As in the first abuse, you funk the issue and put it back for a report. The subcommittee works away and produces its recommendations, only to discover that the principles on which it has been working are entirely unacceptable to the main committee. The Bar Subcommittee devises a highly profitable new price-list only to discover that the Management Committee wanted to subsidise real ale in order to appease the Trotskyites, only nobody dared say it.

LEVELS OF DECISION-MAKING

Alternatively, in the above instance the Bar Subcommittee might not have needed the Management Committee's approval of its price-list. The decision about prices could have been *delegated* to it.

Responsibilities can be delegated from meetings to committees, from committees to subcommittees and from meetings or committees to officers or officials. Then, the body to which responsibilities are delegated has freedom to act – within any limits set. Technically both duties and powers are delegated: the duties to see that something is done; the powers to do it; though often, they are lumped together under the heading of 'functions'.

There are limits to the delegation. No body is usually able to give away all its responsibilities either for political or legal reasons (see 4.2). Thus, the statement of functions for the lower-level body should be clear about the limits

> to manage the social club within the range of activities agreed with the Management Committee
> to commit expenditure on equipment up to £250
> to appoint staff on clerical grades.

The relationship between the body which has delegated the powers and the body to which they are delegated is sometimes sensitive and difficult. I hope it flares up occasionally: if the latter is not trying to push through ideas, it probably isn't working at full steam; if it is producing ideas, these ideas ought to be strong enough sometimes to conflict with the higher-level body.

Whose problem?
An association has to consider what job is best done at what level. Whose problem is it? The principle of delegation is:

– responsibilities should be put on the people and places in the organisation which can most effectively undertake them within the aims and resources of the whole organisation.

This is qualified by two principles:
– responsibilities should be delegated as near the action as possible;
– the structure of responsibilities should be kept as simple and straightforward as possible.

These two principles can conflict. The first suggests that responsibilities should be passed down through an organisation as low as possible. The second suggests retaining responsibilities in one place, and this probably means in the superior body which cannot absolve itself of its responsibilities. Therefore the extent of delegation depends on the particular body. There is no point in a small community group delegating functions to a mass of subcommittees, but equally there is no point in, say, a local education committee not delegating detailed functions to its subcommittees and school governing bodies.

The structures of delegation vary, but generally there is a

hierarchy from the more formal meetings to more relaxed committees and fairly informal subcommittees. These differences can be exploited in the cause of effective meetings. A subcommittee thrives on open-ended discussions between experts or wild, imaginative outbursts but is wrecked by entrenched positions, whereas the reverse may be so of the formal meeting. A subcommittee draws in different people, facts and views on issues which can help formulate a sensible recommendation on which a main committee can put a stamp of legitimacy and the muscle to get something to happen.

Uses and abuses
So I suggest another process for effective meetings. Don't try to run everything in one meeting; sort out which committees and officers should do what and how functions should be delegated to them; set the lines and limits of accountability. If Bar Subcommittee has powers delegated to it to fix prices, the unending wrangle about the mark-up on bitter lemon can be referred to it from the Management Committee, which has got more important issues to think about.

So, one subcommittee reports

> As instructed by . . . , we have . . . .

or

> Within the powers delegated to this subcommittee, we have . . . .

Another subcommittee reports

> According to our terms of reference . . . , we have investigated . . . .
> The facts are . . . .
> The issues are . . . .
> The constraints are . . . .
> We recommend . . . .

And an officer or member of staff reports

> As instructed by the last meeting . . . .
> The situation now is . . . .

But this process also produces two effects which work to the advantage of a controlling group in a committee or association.

First, it makes what happens rather more predictable. Particularly the chair and the most active members have a pretty shrewd idea of what is coming up in reports; more than that, they have helped write them or been close to the people who have. They can prepare a response, foresee the development of a discussion, plot how a decision will be taken. They can fix the interaction that takes place in the meeting – old committee hands do it instinctively.

A controlling group bounces around reports and their recommendations with the ease of the Harlem Globetrotters. Show the other members the issue; flip it to the chair of finance subcommittee; a couple of bounces for the rest to catch up; 'That's helpful', says the chair; over to Dolly with the astute midfield mind; laid off back to chair of finance ('That's within the budget . . .'); through to a comrade speaking for the first time ('In view of what's been said, shouldn't we . . .'); a decision in the net.

Secondly, you create a structure of committees which is no more than a shadow of how and where decisions are actually made. An outsider speaks up in Executive Council

> I want to make the case for people to be happy . . . . This committee never talks about . . . .

The chair replies

> Right on. That's the function of Entertainments Committee.

Off he goes to Entertainments Committee

> I want to make the case . . . .

The chair of Entertainments Committee (who plays squash with the chair of Executive Council) welcomes his statement

> This is really important. What we need from you is a paper setting out your ideas . . . . Or perhaps we could set up a subcommittee . . . . On the other hand, Frank, is this something Positive Experiences Subcommittee would say came under their terms of reference?

The outsider in this example is tough and sticks at it, producing a lengthy paper with snappy recommendations which is hailed as the sort of thing Positive Experiences Subcommittee have been waiting for since 1968.

But, it so happens that the chairs of this Executive Council, Entertainments Committee and Positive Experiences subcommittee meet in a completely different committee structure, and as they are packing up their papers after the White Elephant Management Committee Frank chuckles

Hey, you remember that guy who wanted to talk about happiness. It's coming up on your agenda in a fortnight. What do you think?

They sew it up. It's the people who sit in the web of the committees who make the decisions. Note: (1) they always have another committee where the real discussion was actually taking place; (2) the power is in the hands of the people who make the connections between the committees.

Fortunately, none of these processes can be relied upon to work. Explosions of outrage can seldom be shunted off down the subcommittee lines.

KINDS OF DECISIONS

Which decisions are made at which levels of an association depend on its organisation and habits. In one the general meeting is the all-powerful decision-maker; its toughly-fought debates lead to resolutions which set strong lines of policy and specify how they are to be implemented. In another the general meeting approves the executive committee's report on the year, elects the executive for another year, approves the annual accounts and has a beano. In one association the executive committee issues detailed instructions to officers; in another it lets the officers work within very wide guidelines. One subcommittee has delegated powers; another can only advise. A member of staff may not be able to write a letter without authorisation from the committee; another association may be in the staff's pocket.

From meeting to meeting in thinking about levels and kinds of decisions we face such nice political judgement as:

– how do I save my own skin?;
– do we need to cover ourselves by getting the meeting's approval?;
– shall I leave the treasurer to be torn limb from limb?;
– will they ever trust us again?

But there are more general and more public criteria. On the one hand:

– the amount of principle involved in a decision, or the precedents which it establishes;
– the generality of the decision, or the size of its impâct;
– its newness;
– its political sensitivity (does it ring alarm bells?).

On the other hand:

– its technical or professional or merely administrative nature;
– its continuation of existing policies;
– its being an implementation of a previous decision;
– its pettiness, its triviality.

Decisions weighted towards the first group are more likely to be kept higher in an organisation or to an association's main committee. Decisions weighted towards the second may be put to a lower tier of subcommittees, entrusted to officers or unloaded on staff. In such a way we tend to distinguish between policy decisions and administrative or professional decisions.

For our own associations we have to develop the sense of what kind of decision goes where. For instance, what kind of decisions should our executive committee make? It depends on:

– the weight of the decision as between policy and administration, as above;
– the amount of detail required, as I discussed previously about issuing instructions.

Suppose: a politically shifting situation; sensitive negotiations approaching; a committee that can't be together day and night; officers or staff who will have to act for us, though we find that if we give them a lot of rope they hang us. We have to formulate our decisions in terms of:

– our intentions;
– any imperatives in how they are to be achieved;
– constraints, resources and manpower;
– what we would regard as a successful achievement of our intentions;
– who is to take what responsibility;
– the authorisation to act.

Some powerful committees are like traffic lights:

– red, that is a crummy proposal;
– amber, come back when you have worked it out again;
– green, we authorise you to go in that direction and (adding a direction sign) to keep going until you reach the High Street, then turn left (or right, or ask again).

For all the ins-and-outs of procedure and the complexities of politics, committees and meetings are simple control devices. (And, for all the mystery, it takes people to operate them.)

5.3 POLITICS

All over the place people are ruining the reputation of democracy by holding committees and meetings. Not that they are always running them badly, inept at procedure or unskilful in handling people. They are holding meetings for the wrong reasons.

It's too much effort to make a decision now. Let's get a committee to look into it.

Damn, Stevie has turned up. Now we certainly can't discuss setting up a vigilante corps. Tell you what: let's set up a working party on safety in the streets.

It's five to ten. We're too tired to make up our minds now. Set up a subcommittee.

I daren't suggest staff redundancies. I'll get a committee to create a smokescreen.

Committees and meetings are special mechanisms or institutions
which we can deploy when we need them. They are not forced on
us by a deity. They are not the earthly echoes of Tolkien-like
struggles between the forces of collectivism and individualism by
which we are helplessly buffeted.

We decide to use these devices for a purpose. We might have
preferred to form an unstructured group or an organisation with
different rules. We could have acted through individual executive
decision. We could have made a telephone call, held a seminar or
T-group, sent a letter, met over a pint or a coffee.

Consider a group of allies meeting without a procedural
structure. The advantages of that *might* be:

- honesty of feeling, directness of points of view;
- open gathering of ideas, brainstorming;
- raising consciousness of problems and issues;
- probing around and around a subject;
- freedom from rigmarole;
- intensity and strength of response to external attack, un-
  constrained by procedure for turning ideas and feeling into
  motions and amendments;
- a group loyalty, supportive to those already members but
  hostile to outsiders and different points of view;
- flexibility, meeting when people like, working on personal trust,
  not needing authorisations and written records;
- elusiveness from established structures of society, police and
  state.

There might be difficulties in coping with different points of view
and other kinds of people, in articulating decisions so that the
group can check later whether it has done what it meant to do, in
keeping up consistent pressure, in maintaining continuity after its
leaders move on.

But we choose for some purposes the more formal structure of
meetings and committees because we want to make use of its
advantages:

- bringing together different factions and points of view;
- providing procedure for fair debate;
- providing procedure for managing complex business and
  coming to clearly stated decisions;

— maintaining a continuing organisation and existence;
— securing legitimacy, agreement and solidarity;
— fitting into a structure of decision-making and accountability.

Suppose, as an outline example: a campaign against the location of a new industrial plant. We can choose our form of action.

If we want: anger turned straight into action from people who trust each other and feel united; a campaign which is direct and simple — 'It must be stopped'; a group of campaigners who are concerned about their own integrity of ideas and responses; shock — our opponents finding us unpredictable; spontaneity; we would probably not be helped by forming a committee working with conventional procedure.

If we want: different interests and groups to come together — political leaders and ecologists, teachers and liberation movements, experts and citizens, trades council and small shopkeepers; a sustained and public campaign; negotiations across the table with the directors of the industry and with government and its agencies; orchestrated public meetings and demonstrations; proposals for alternative uses of the site which command a wide base of support; we probably would find it useful to form a committee and formal structure.

Within the campaign we might go through different phases: a furious, unstructured outburst, followed by deliberating committees; and maybe our committee continue to use the threat of unleashing the ecologists as a negotiating tactic. The distinctions are not absolute: our committee from one meeting to the next might be like a group of friends, but we can always change mode and snap into the formal processes of power.

What distinguishes the committee structure from the less formal group is that it operates in public:

1. We connect to other structures of power and administration. We have a representative of the council on our committee, or we use our legitimacy and public support as a committee to negotiate with the council.

2. We are a body which other bodies can deal with. We have a continuing existence, a constitutional or legal status, and we are recognised. The trade union, the leader of the council, the soccer club, the charitable foundation, the other local bodies, they know whom to come to.

3. We owe our position to the people and other bodies who

have elected or appointed us (or sanctioned us) to act on their behalf. We are accountable to them.

Accountability

We are not on this committee because of our personal brilliance and razor-sharp minds. We are here because other people and other bodies have decided to trust us to act for them. True, we schemed and slaughtered to get here, to be noticed as among the great and the good, the ambitious and the servile, but technically, realistically we owe our positions to them. So, we are accountable to them, accountable twice-over, for political honesty and for survival. We operate under their scrutiny; though what we do in the depths of a committee room may be hidden, we report back; we represent their views and interests (see 1.3); they might even be able to recall us and vote us out of office; then the crunch, we stand for re-election.

Committees and formal meetings are mechanisms for account-ability. They connect people and associations in a political relationship, in discussions and decisions about what people say should happen and about the power to make it. As mechanisms of democracy they are not infallible: we spend months not bothering about our constituency; the members' interest comes in spas-modic rushes; we manoeuvre to control elections and retain personal power. But at rock-bottom the structure every so often brings decisions into the open and gives other people and alternative ideas the opportunity to be heard. We can improve our use of these processes.

At least, tonight perhaps we could get through the business in two hours.

References

Auld, R. (1976). *William Tyndale Junior and Infants Schools Public Inquiry*. London: Inner London Education Authority.

Citrine, Lord (1952). *ABC of chairmanship*. Third edition. London: NCLC Publishing Society.

Denning, Lord (1979). *The discipline of law*. London: Butterworths.

Goodman Report (1976). *Charity law and voluntary organisations*. London: Bedford Square Press, NCSS.

Josling, J. F. and Alexander, L. (1975). *The law of clubs*. Third edition. London: Oyez.

Lidderdale, Sir David (1976). *Erskine May's Treatise on the law, privileges, proceedings and usage of parliament*. London: Butterworths.

Nathan Report (1950). *Law and practice relating to charitable trusts*. London: HMSO.

Nightingale, B. (1973). *Charities*. London: Allen Lane.

Palgrave, R. F. D. (1964). *The chairman's handbook*. Revised by Abraham, L. A. London: Dent.

Pateman, C. (1970). *Participation and democratic theory*. Cambridge: Cambridge University Press.

Perrins, R. E. G. and Jeffreys, A. (1970). *Ranking and Spicer's Company law*. London: HFL (Publishers).

Stevenson, D. (1972). *50 million volunteers*. London: HMSO.

Strauss, B. W. and Strauss, F. (1966). *New ways to better meetings*. London: Social Science Paperbacks, Associated Book Publishers.

Taylor Report (1977). *A new partnership for our schools*. London: HMSO.

Wade, E. C. S. and Phillips, G. G. (1977). *Constitutional and administrative law*. Ninth edition by Bradley, A. W. London: Longman.

Further reading

Citrine, Lord (1952). *ABC of chairmanship*. Third edition. London: NCLC Publishing Society. Authoritative textbook on procedure, aimed particularly at trade unions and the Labour movement.

Clarke, S. (1978). *Working on a committee*. London: Community Projects Foundation. Brief guide to organising community associations, based on discussion of people's motivation and skills.

Hannington, W. (1950). *Mr Chairman!* London: Lawrence and Wishart. Like Citrine, aimed at the Labour movement, but shorter and more comradely.

Hayes, D. (1974). *Keeping accounts: A handbook for voluntary organisations*. London: Bedford Square Press, National Council of Social Service. Practical booklet on keeping accounts and the treasurer's role.

Hayes, J. (editor) (1978). *How to run a tenants' association*. Sixth edition. London: Association of London Housing Estates. Organising social events and fund-raising, producing a newsletter etc., as well as brief note about committees and a specimen constitution.

Hunt, J. (1977). *Point of order*. Nuneaton: National Association of Youth Clubs. Introductory booklet, aimed at youth clubs.

Sladen, E. (1978). *Honorary officers and what they do*. London: Bedford Square Press, National Council of Social Service. Advice on being chairman, secretary, treasurer.

Smith, J. and Pearse, M. (1977). *How community groups work*. London: Community Projects Foundation. Bright, brief and sharp discussion of allocating work, organising committees and groups etc., part of a set of 'Community Groups Handbooks'.

Useful leaflets and more specialist handbooks are published by:

Community Projects Foundation, 7 Leonard Street, London EC2 4AQ.
National Council of Social Service, 26 Bedford Square, London WC1B 3HU.
Association for Neighbourhood Councils, PO Box 1, Halstead, Essex.

Legal framework:
Grant, L., Hewitt, P., Jackson, C. and Levenson, H. (1978). *Civil liberty: The NCCL guide to your rights*. Third edition. Harmondsworth: Penguin.
Josling, J. F. and Alexander, L. (1975). *The law of clubs*. Third edition. London: Oyez.
Street, H. (1977). *Freedom, the individual and the law*. Fourth edition. Harmondsworth: Penguin.

Charity law:
Cracknell, D. G. (1973). *The law relating to charities*. London: Oyez.
Picarda, H. (1977). *The law and practice relating to charities*. London: Butterworths.

Glossary and index

Abstention, voting neither for nor against – because you can't decide or because you have decided neither side should be supported.

Ad hoc committee, committee set up for a particular task, a special committee. See 2.1, 5.2. For dealing with their reports, see 3.10.

Adjourn, break off a meeting to resume it later – maybe after a few minutes, maybe some days, maybe specifically a week. For members' ways of proposing, see 3.11. For chair's power, see 3.12.

Agenda, list of business to be discussed. For organisation and styles, see 3.3. For secretary's skills in drawing up, see 2.3. For chair's handling, see 2.2.

Amendment, a change proposed to a motion. See 3.6. As a tactic, see 2.6.

Annual accounts, statement of income and expenditure for the year, to be audited and approved by the annual general meeting. For treasurer's role, see 2.4. For legal importance, see 4.1. For secretary's responsibility, see 2.3.

Annual general meeting (AGM), annual meeting of association which, usually, elects a committee and officers, approves the annual report and annual accounts, appoints auditors for the coming year and debates policy. See 2.1, 3.1.

Annual report, report on year's activities by the chair, committee or chief executive.

Any other business (AOB), item at end of agenda to sweep up business not on the rest of the agenda. Major and controversial business cannot, usually, be raised here. See 3.3.

Apologies for absence, the secretary reports at the beginning of the meeting whom has apologised for being unable to attend. See 3.1. For place on agenda, see 3.3.

Articles of association, document setting out the conduct of a company, including shareholders' rights.

Articles of government, document setting out the conduct of a governing body, including powers and duties of governing body, headteacher (schools), principal (colleges), academic board (colleges) etc.

Auditors, accountants (appointed by AGM) to check that the annual accounts are a true representation of the financial situation.

Ballot, a vote, usually on paper voting slips (rather than by show of hands).

Block vote, a 'card vote'. See 3.8.

Call to order, chair says 'I call the meeting to order' to start a meeting or, during the meeting, to tell members to behave properly.

Card vote, vote which counts the numbers in the associations represented at the meeting (rather than the numbers of representative present). See 3.8.

Casting vote, the chair can often cast a vote to resolve a tie. See 3.8.

Catch the chair's eye, conventional explanation of how the chair selects speakers – by noticing you raise your hand etc. For chair's task, see 2.2. For ordinary member's position, see 2.6.

Chair's action, power of chair to act on routine or urgent matters between meetings. See 2.2.

Challenge to the chair, to try to overturn the chair's ruling. See 3.11.

Charity, body recognised as charitable by Charity Commissioners and/or Inland Revenue. See 4.2.

Clerk, see 'secretary', 2.3.

Committee, group of people appointed or elected to do a job. For technical differences between 'committee' and 'meeting', see 1.1 and 3.1.

Composite (motion), motion combining several motions on the same topic. See 3.6.

Confidentiality, see 3.1.

Constitution, statement of the objects and conduct of an association. It is sometimes used more narrowly to refer just to the composition of a committee. See 1.2, 3.1. For distribution of powers and officers' responsibilities, see 2.1.

Coopted (member), member appointed to a committee by the

people who are already on the committee. See 2.1. For voting rights, see 3.8.

Correspondence, item on agenda when secretary reads out the mail. For secretary's task, see 2.3. For place on agenda, see 3.3.

Declaration of interest, statement that you are personally involved – usually financially – in the issue being discussed. See 3.1.

Delegate, person sent by an association or group to represent it at another meeting. A 'delegate' (as distinct from a 'representative') can be instructed how to vote by his or her constituency. See 1.3.

Delegated powers, powers handed down to a committee or officer to act on behalf of the higher level committee or meeting. 'Delegated powers' enable the lower level body to act (rather than simply make recommendations to the higher level body). See 2.1, 5.2.

Dilatory motion, motion like 'next business' or 'previous question' that postpones or delays a decision.

Disruption, see 3.12.

Drafting amendment, amendment that tidies up wording of a motion.

Election, see 3.9. Of officers and committee, see 2.1. For secretary's task, see 2.3.

Emergency motion, a motion which was not on the agenda but is discussed because it is urgent and relates to fresh events. See 3.6.

Exhaustive ballot, see 3.8.

Ex officio, put on a committee because of an office or post which you hold. See 3.1.

Formally second, the seconder can 'formally second' a motion, not making a speech at the beginning of the debate and thereby reserving the chance of speaking later. See 3.6.

Gavel, chair's hammer. He or she bangs it to call the meeting to order.

General meeting, meeting of all members. Each year there is an 'annual general meeting'. In addition, 'special' or 'extraordinary' general meetings can be called, often if requested by a specific number of members, to make decisions on major issues. For secretary's task, see 2.3. For provision in constitution, see 2.1, 3.2.

Guillotine, decision taken in advance that a debate will be cut off at a particular time.

Instrument of government, document which sets out the existence and composition of a governing body.

Mandate, usually refers to something which you are commanded to do. Delegates may be 'mandated' to vote for one side.

Matters arising, item on agenda for reporting on topics which appear in the minutes of the previous meeting and which are not on the agenda for this meeting. See 3.3.

Memorandum of association, document setting out the existence and powers of a company, including its objects and range of activities.

Minutes, record of meeting. See 3.4. For secretary's task, see 2.3. For dealing with subcommittee minutes, see 3.10.

Motion, formal proposal to be debated. See 3.6.

Motion be put, as 'question be put'. See 3.7.

Nem con, no-one disagrees. But someone abstains – otherwise it would be 'unanimous'.

Next business, motion which interrupts meeting to propose that it stops discussing a topic *and* does not vote on it. See 3.7. As tactic, see 2.6.

Notice (of meeting), see 3.2. For secretary's task, see 2.3.

Objects clause, the statement in a constitution of the purpose of an association. It often comes as the second paragraph (the first being the association's name). See 3.1. For charitable nature, see 4.2. In relation to ultra vires, see 3.1, 3.6, 4.2.

'Order. Order', how some chairs start a meeting or get its members to behave properly.

Out of order, the chair can declare a motion 'out of order' for being ultra vires or for not being in accordance with rules or standing orders, see 3.6. The chair can tell members they are 'out of order' for speaking or behaving improperly, see 3.1, 3.12.

Point of information, device to interrupt a meeting to correct or supplement what a speaker is saying. See 3.11.

Point of order, device for members to check the conduct and progress of a meeting. See 3.11. As tactic, see 2.6.

Poll, vote, usually same as 'card vote'. See 3.8.

Previous business, device to propose that the topic should not be discussed. See 3.7.

Proportional representation, see 3.8.

Proposer, person (or delegation) who proposes the motion (or amendment) and speaks first. See 3.6.

Proxy, vote cast by one person on behalf of someone else. See 3.8.

Question be put, motion which interrupts meeting to propose that the vote should be taken at once. See 3.7.

Quorum, minimum number who must be present at meeting. See 3.5. For place in constitution, see 3.1.

Reference back, the meeting can decide to hand back a report from a committee, subcommittee or officer and ask them to think again; often it amounts to a polite rejection. See 3.10. As tactic, see 2.6.

Remit to executive, rather than proceeding to vote for or against a motion (including a motion to accept or approve a report and its recommendations), the meeting can decide to put the motion to the executive committee to consider what to do. See 3.6, 3.10.

Report, for dealing with, see 3.10 and 5.2. For secretary's task, see 2.3.

Resolution, strictly speaking, a motion which has been approved by the meeting, but frequently it is used, rather incorrectly, interchangeably with 'motion'. See 3.6.

Rulebook, document setting out the constitution and rules.

Seconder, person (or delegation) who is the principal supporter of the proposer, speaking immediately after the proposer or after the opposer (if any), unless he or she 'formally seconds'. A seconder is not usually required in committees, see 3.1. See 3.6.

Single transferable vote, see 3.8.

Slate, list of candidates for election being supported by one faction.

Special committee, committee set up to undertake a particular, short-term task. See 2.1. For dealing with reports, see 3.10, 5.2.

Standing committee, committee set up to deal with regular and continuing business. See 2.1. For dealing with reports, see 3.10, 5.2.

Standing orders, rules by which meetings are conducted, often just the detailed rules (as distinct from the major principles which are set out in the constitution, instrument and articles etc.). See 1.2, 3.1.

Subcommittee, a committee set up by a committee. See 2.1. For dealing with reports, see 3.10, 5.2.

Substantive motion, the main motion (as distinct from amendments proposed to it). After amendments have been carried, the amended motion is often called the 'substantive motion', as when the chair says 'We have dealt with the amendment, and now we turn to the substantive motion'. See 3.6.

Summing-up, or 'right of reply', see 3.6.

Suspend standing orders, a standing order which is obstructing the wish of the meeting can be suspended in special circumstances. See 3.11.

Taken in parts, a motion can be voted on section-by-section. See 3.6.

Teller, person who counts the votes.

Terms of reference, what a committee, subcommittee or working party has been set up to do. See 2.1.

Trustee, see 4.2.

Two-thirds majority, see 3.8.

Ultra vires, outside the powers of the association, committee or officer. See 4.2. In relation to 'out of order' motions, see 3.6. In relation to general principles, see 2.1, 3.1.

Unanimous, everyone present agrees.

Unincorporated association, see 4.2.

Vote, see 3.8. For elections, see 3.9.